Key Stage 3 Science Support

Science

Ages 11–12

Bob McDuell and Graham Booth

survival GUIDE

Letts Educational
Chiswick Centre
414 Chiswick High Road
London W4 5TF
Tel: 020 8996 3333
Fax: 020 8996 8390
Email: mail@lettsed.co.uk
Website: www.letts-education.com

First published 2003

10 9 8 7 6 5 4 3 2

British Library Cataloging in Publication Data. A CIP record of this book is available from the British Library.

ISBN 1 84315 114 6

Letts Educational Limited is a division of Granada Learning Limited, part of the Granada Media Group.

Edited and typeset by Cambridge Publishing Management

Designed by Moondisks Limited

Science

Book 1 Ages 11–12

1

From primary to secondary

Most pupils enjoy science at primary school and look forward to studying science at secondary school.

At secondary school:

- science is studied in specially-equipped rooms called laboratories, or 'labs' for short
- there are opportunities to carry out more experiments using specialist equipment
- science is taught by teachers who usually only teach science, so they are 'experts'.

Key Stage 2 to Key Stage 3

As you progress through the first three years of science at secondary school, called Key Stage 3, you should:

- learn about more scientific processes
- improve your understanding about how and why things happen
- develop scientific skills such as reasoning, investigating and problem-solving.

What will I study?

In each year of secondary school, you will study a number of different scientific topics. These will probably be broken down into small chunks called 'units' or 'modules'.

In Year 7, some of these topics may be new to you, for example a study of acids and alkalis. Other topics, such as electricity, will build on work that you have already done at primary school.

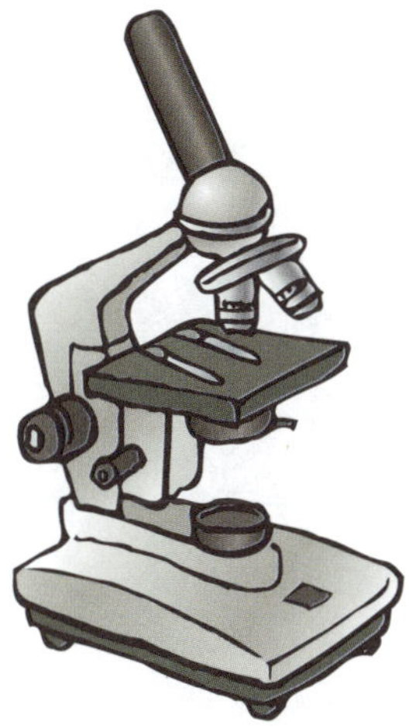

Each topic that you study will come from one of three main areas of science:

- biology – this is the study of all living things, such as plants and animals
- chemistry – this is the study of materials, their reactions and their uses
- physics – this is concerned with how we use things such as electricity, light and sound.

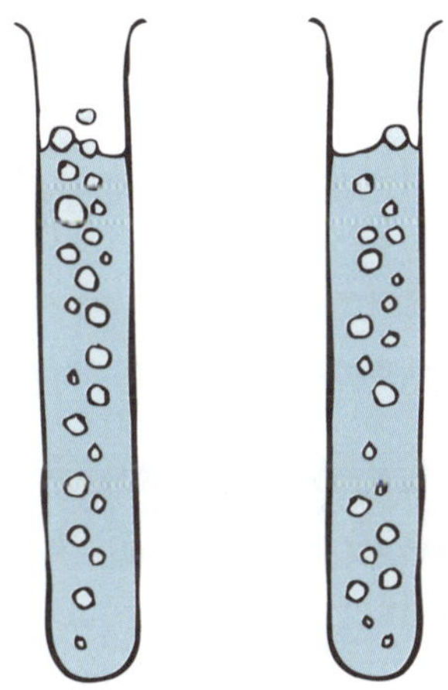

Will there be tests?

Normally, you can expect to be tested at the end of each unit of study. These tests will assess:

- what you have learned – including the meaning of scientific terms
- your understanding – how well you can explain scientific processes
- your scientific skills – for example in analysing data from experiments.

Using this Survival Guide should help to make sure that you do your best in all your science tests and examinations.

What are cells?

Just as a house is built out of bricks, animals and plants are made out of cells. Cells are the building blocks of all living things.

There are differences between the cells that make up animals and those that make up plants. The diagram shows typical plant and animal cells.

There is a key difference between plant cells and animal cells – plant cells have a cell wall.

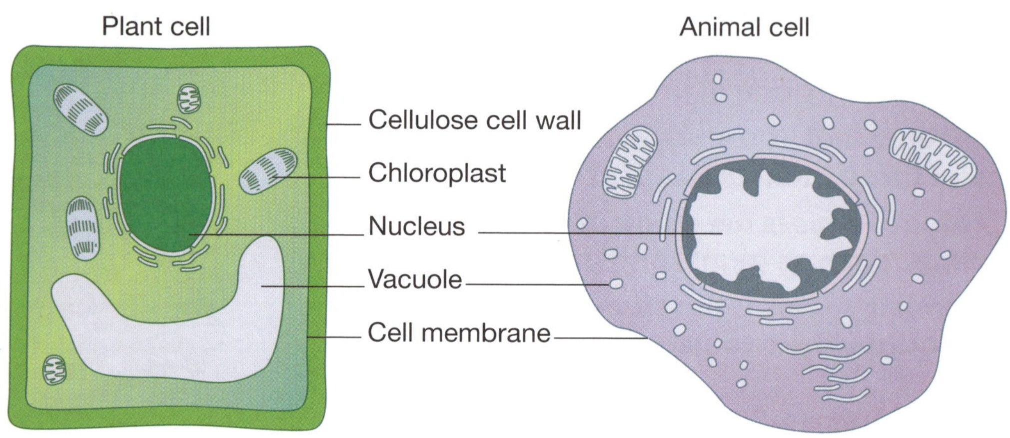

Animals have a skeleton to keep them in shape. Their cells are soft to the touch.

Plants do not have a skeleton – they stay upright because they have a tough wall around each cell. This cell wall is made from a chemical called cellulose.

Exercise 1

1 Which two things found in plant cells are not found in animal cells?

2 Explain why a plant cell is harder to squash than an animal cell.

3 What are plant cell walls made from?

4 The diagram shows a cell from a human cheek.

Write down the names of the parts labelled A, B and C.

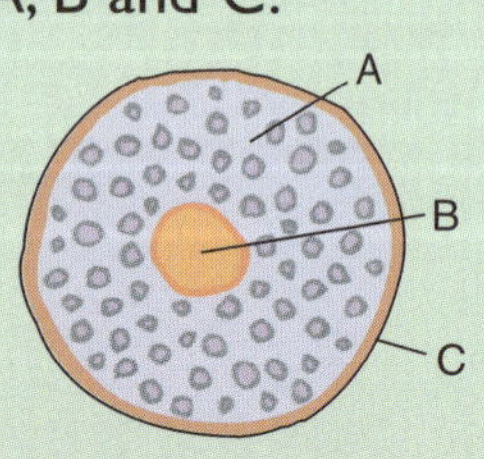

Tactics

Questions about the differences between plant and animal cells are common in tests at Key Stage 3.

RED ALERT Plant cells have cell walls – animal cells do not. RED ALERT

Cells in plants and animals

Most cells have:

- a nucleus that controls the actions of the cell
- cytoplasm – a mixture of chemicals that includes nutrition that has passed into the cell and waste products on their way out of the cell
- a cell membrane – this holds the cell together and allows nutrients to pass in and waste products to pass out.

Some cells, such as mature red blood cells, do not have a nucleus.

In addition, most plant cells have:

- chloroplasts – these contain a green chemical called chlorophyll that absorbs energy from the Sun. This energy is needed for the plant to make food
- a cell wall to keep the cell in shape.

Cells in the roots of plants do not have chloroplasts. As they are not exposed to sunlight, they cannot make food, so chloroplasts are not needed.

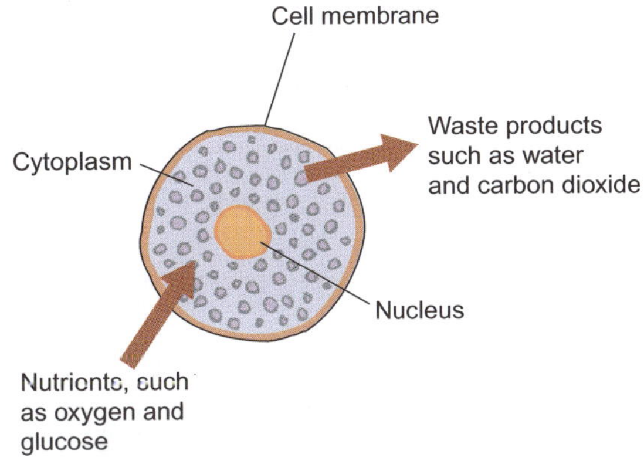

Exercise 2

1 Which part of a cell controls its actions?

2 Explain why the cell membrane needs to allow substances to pass in and out of the cell.

3 Which chemical absorbs the energy for plants to make food?

4 Explain why the leaves of most plants are green, but their roots are not.

5 What substances are found in the cytoplasm of a cell?

Tactics

Remember that cell membranes and cell walls allow substances to pass through them in both directions.

Building with cells

Building with cells

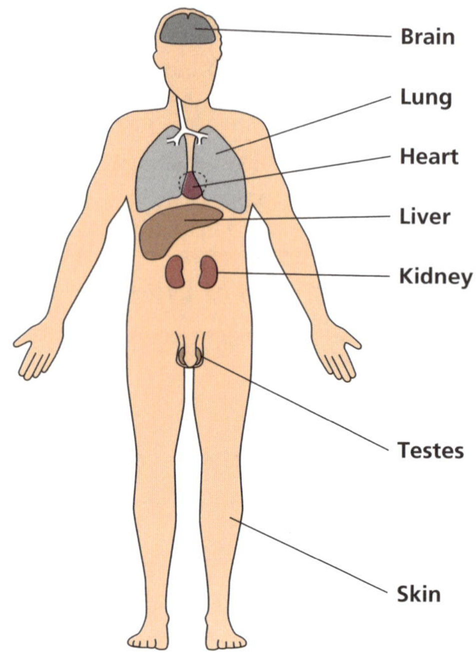

There are lots of different types of cell that make up an animal or plant.

A body organ such as the heart or lung has a certain job to do. The diagram shows some of the organs that make up a human male body.

Each organ is made up of one or more different types of tissue, these are groups of cells that carry out a similar task. The more complex the organ, the more different types of tissue there are.

- Cells of the same type are grouped together to make tissue such as muscle or nerve.
- All the cells in a tissue carry out a similar task.
- Several different tissues are normally used to make up an organ.

> Cells make tissue and tissue makes organs. A group of organs that work together is called an organ system.

Cells e.g. nerve cells → Tissues e.g. nerve tissues → Organs e.g. brain → Systems e.g. nervous system →

Exercise 1

1. What is tissue made up of?
2. What are organs made up of?
3. Which organ shown in the diagram:
   - a pumps blood around the body?
   - b exchanges gases with the air?
   - c controls the actions of the body?
   - d is part of the reproductive system?

Tactics

Remember that an organ system is a group of organs that work together to carry out a task.

RED ALERT Cells make tissue. Tissues make organs. Organs make organ systems. **RED ALERT**

Different tissues

Your body is made up of a number of organs, each of which has a different job. An organ is in turn made up of different kinds of tissue.

Some important organs are:

- the eye – this contains muscle tissue to move the eyeball, nerve tissue to send information to the brain and connective tissue that forms the 'white' of the eye
- the skin – this contains nerve tissue, sweat gland tissue and blood vessel tissue
- the heart – this contains lining tissue, tendon tissue and connective tissue.

These diagrams show some of the tissues in the eye and skin.

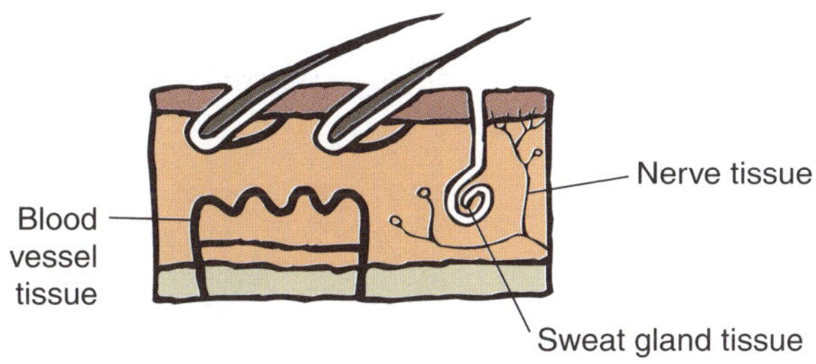

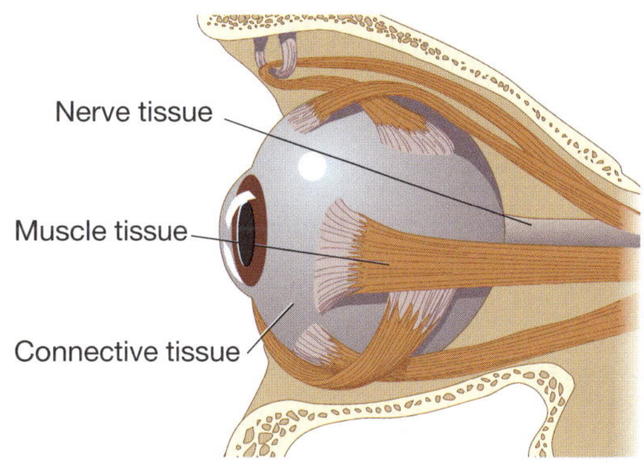

You can see how organs are made of different types of tissue, each of which has a different job to do within the organ.

Plants also have different types of tissue that do special jobs. Inside the stem of a plant the phloem tissue transports food and minerals both up and down the stem. Water from the roots moves through the xylem tissue up the stem to all parts of the plant.

Exercise 2

1 What is the job of nerve tissue?

2 What is the job of muscle tissue in the eye?

3 Explain why an organ such as the eye needs different types of tissue.

4 Explain why you would expect to find a lot of muscle tissue in the arms and legs.

Tactics

Remember that each type of tissue in an organ has a different job.

Specialised cells

Cells in different tissues have different jobs to do. Their shape is adapted so that they can do their job efficiently.

The diagrams below show some specialised cells and how they are adapted to do a certain job.

A leaf is an important organ of a plant. It exchanges gases with the atmosphere, absorbs energy from the Sun and makes food. Different types of tissue are needed to carry out these jobs. Different types of cells are needed to make up the different tissues in a leaf.

A cell from the upper surface of a leaf has lots of chloroplasts to absorb energy from the Sun.

Cells in the underneath part of a leaf have very few chloroplasts.

This root hair cell has no chloroplasts – it is underground. It has a large surface area so that water and minerals can pass into the cell.

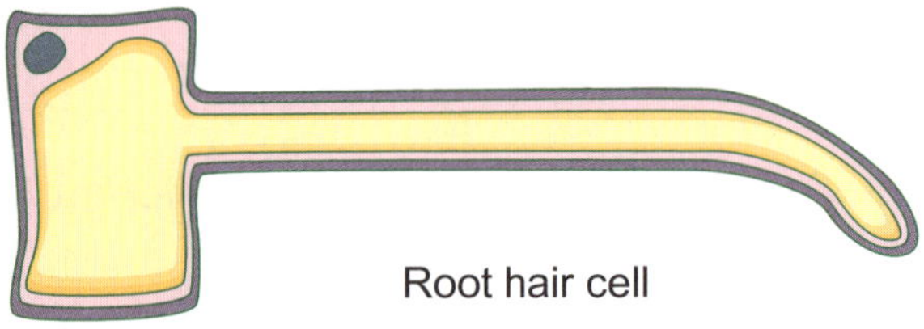

Root hair cell

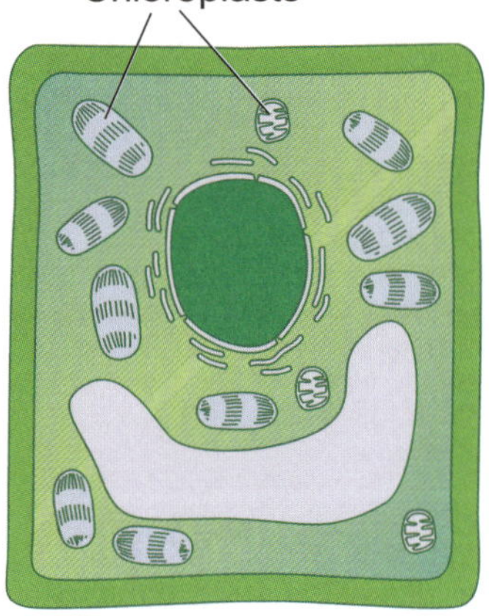

Cell from a leaf

The tissues that make up the stem and the roots have yet different jobs to do, so, again, other types of cells are needed to make up these tissues.

Exercise 1

1 Explain why the cells in the upper part of a leaf have more chloroplasts than those on the underneath of the leaf.

2 What is the job of a root hair cell?

3 How is a root hair cell adapted to do its job?

4 Why does a root hair cell not need chloroplasts?

Tactics

Questions about different types of plant cell are common in tests at Key Stage 3. Remember that the cells on the upper side of a leaf have more chloroplasts than those on the underneath.

 You need to know about how the cells described on these pages are adapted to do their jobs.

Specialised animal cells

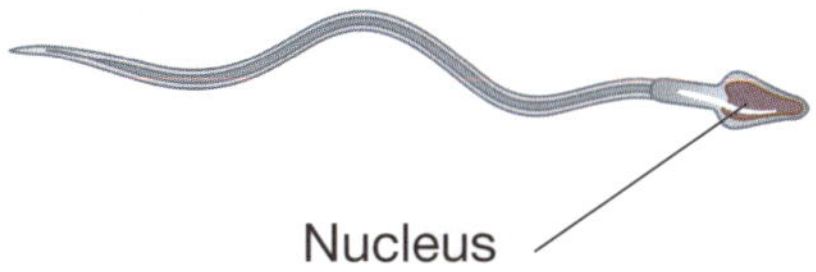

A sperm cell is a male sex cell. It needs to travel a long way so it has a tail to propel it and a streamlined shape.

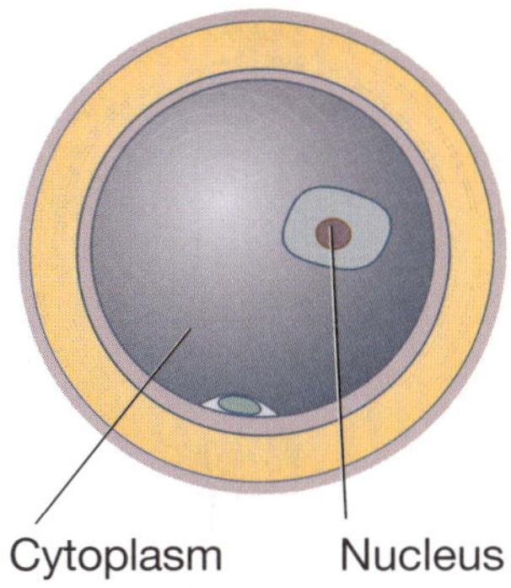

An egg cell or ovum is a female sex cell. It is much bigger than a sperm. It does not have to propel itself.

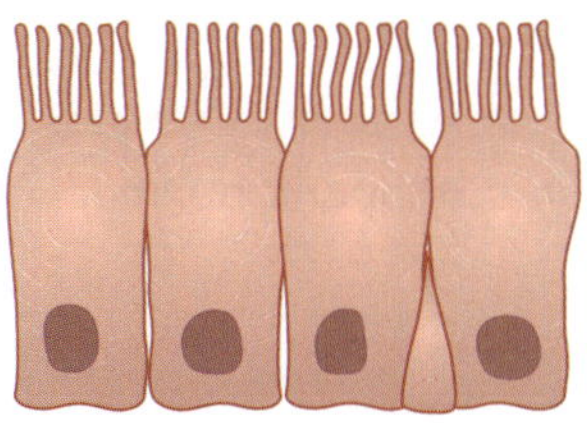

Cells in the trachea or windpipe have tiny hairs called cilia. The job of these hairs is to trap bacteria and dust so they do not enter the lungs.

Making new cells

Plants and animals need to make new cells for growth and repair. As a cell grows it divides into two identical copies of the original cell. When a cell divides:

- the cell nucleus first copies itself
- the two identical nuclei move to opposite ends of the cell
- the cell divides into two parts, with each new cell containing a nucleus.

Exercise 2

1. Which part of the sperm cell contains the nucleus?
2. What is the job of the tail of a sperm cell?
3. Explain why egg cells do not have tails.
4. What are cilia?
5. What is the job of cilia?

Tactics

Smoking paralyses the cilia, so they cannot do their job. Heavy smokers are more prone to lung infections.

Reproduction and adolescence

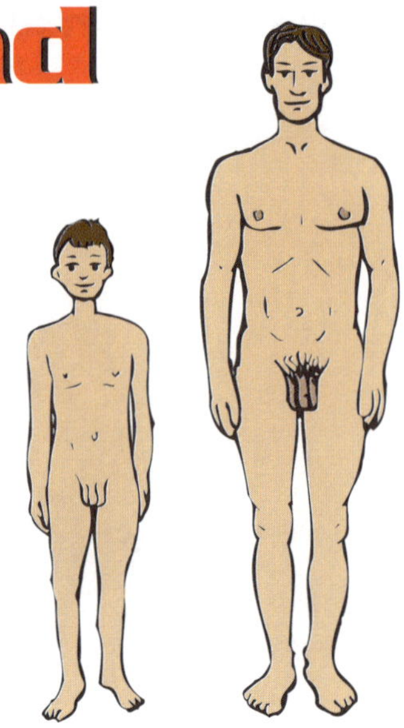

New humans are created by sexual reproduction.

In sexual reproduction a male sex cell joins with a female sex cell to create a new living thing.

Some plants and animals can reproduce without sex. This is called asexual reproduction.

An example of asexual reproduction is growing a new plant by taking a cutting from an existing plant.

Before they can reproduce, children need to change into adults. This happens during adolescence, which takes place in the early teenage years.

Adolescence in boys

In boys the main changes that take place between the ages of eleven and fourteen are:

- male sex cells (sperm) are produced
- the voice becomes deeper
- hair grows around the penis and on the scrotum
- the penis becomes larger.

Exercise 1

1. What is meant by *asexual reproduction*?
2. Which cells join together in sexual reproduction?
3. What happens to an individual male or female during adolescence?
4. Describe the changes that take place to the sex organs of a boy during adolescence.
5. Explain why some plants can reproduce asexually but humans cannot.

Tactics

Sexual reproduction involves two parents – a male and a female. Asexual reproduction is also known as cloning.

RED ALERT Remember the different changes that take place to boys and girls during adolescence. RED A

Adolescence in girls

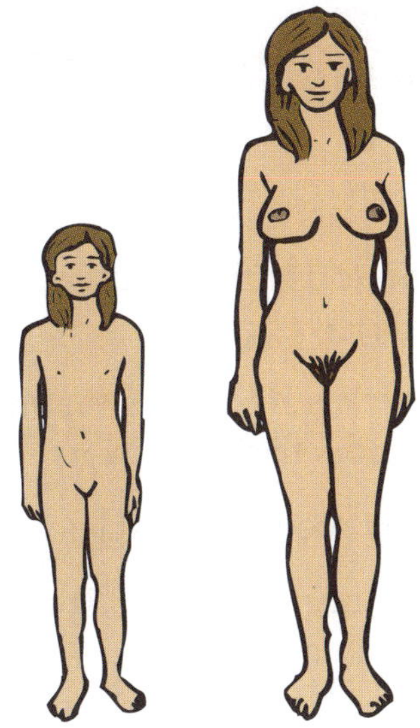

In girls, adolescence may start earlier, from the age of ten.

The main changes that take place are:

- female sex cells (ova) are released from the ovaries
- breasts develop
- hair grows around the vulva, the fleshy external opening to the vagina
- a regular menstrual cycle begins, with periods each month
- the hips broaden, ready for childbirth.

Changes in boys and girls

Both boys and girls change emotionally during adolescence. They become sexually attracted to other people and are often concerned about whether they are sexually attractive to others. They are forever combing their hair and checking their appearance in a mirror.

Controlling the changes

The changes that take place in both boys and girls during adolescence are controlled by special chemicals called hormones.

In boys they are controlled by the hormone testosterone. This is produced by cells in the testes.

In girls they are controlled by the hormone oestrogen, which is produced in the ovaries.

Exercise 2

1 Why do adult females need breasts?

2 How often does a period occur in an adult female?

3 State three external changes that occur to the body of a female during adolescence.

4 Which organs release female sex cells?

5 Explain why teenage boys and girls are often concerned about their appearance.

Tactics

Remember that physical changes are not the only changes that take place during adolescence.

Menstruation

A period is the result of the uterus, or womb, preparing itself each month to receive a fertilised egg.

The diagram shows the main parts of the female reproductive system.

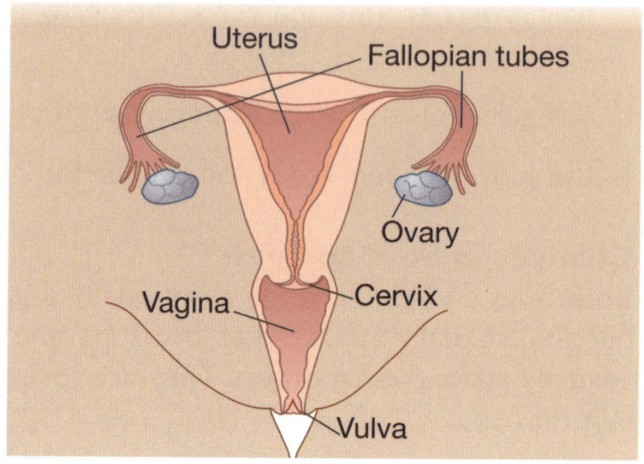

In the menstrual cycle:

- an egg ripens and is released from an ovary each month
- as the egg travels slowly along the fallopian tube, the lining of the uterus thickens
- if the egg enters the uterus unfertilised the thickened lining falls away
- the unfertilised egg and the lining of the uterus pass out through the vagina – this is the period.

One egg at a time

The human female reproductive system is designed to produce and nurture offspring one at a time. Twins are not uncommon but examples of triplets, quadruplets and quintuplets are rare. Non-identical twins result when two eggs are released from the ovaries and both are fertilised. The twins are not identical because they inherit different genetic information from both mother and father.

Exercise 1

1 Which part of the female reproductive system:

  a is the entrance to the uterus from the vagina?

  b releases eggs?

  c prepares itself to receive a fertilised egg?

2 What happens to the uterus during a period?

3 What other name is commonly used for the uterus?

4 Describe how an egg reaches the uterus after being released from an ovary.

Tactics

Remember that menstruation occurs when the thickened lining of the uterus passes out through the vagina.

RED ALERT The menstrual cycle is called a cycle because it keeps repeating itself. Each cycle lasts about one month. RED ALERT

Most humans do not have a twin brother or sister. This is because normally a single egg is released each month from just one of the ovaries. If this egg is fertilised, it is not competing for food and nutrients as it develops.

Stages in the menstrual cycle

This diagram shows the changes that take place during the menstrual cycle.

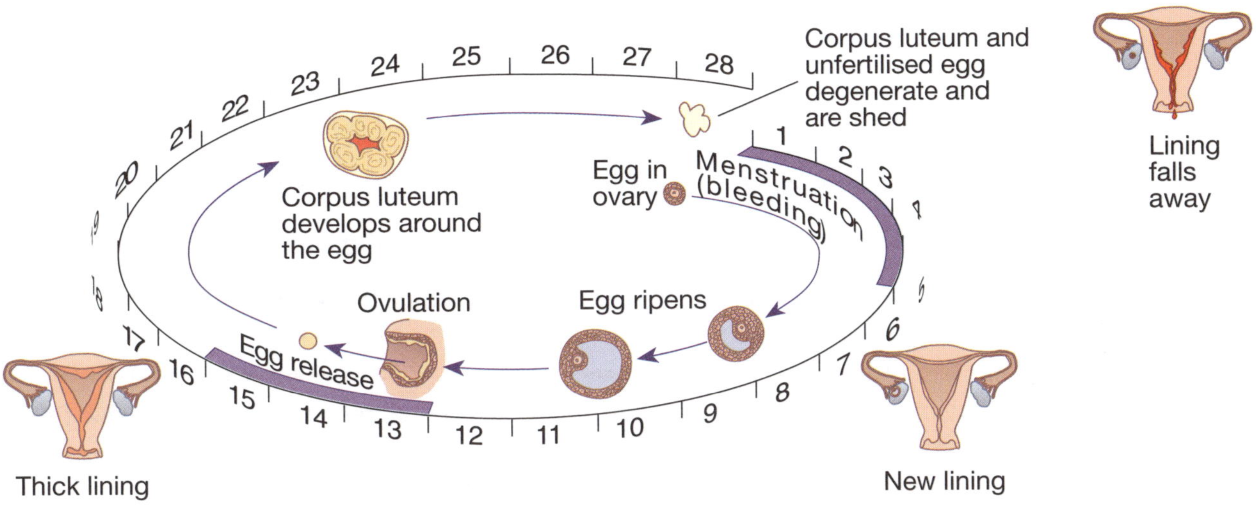

These changes are controlled by the hormones oestrogen, which causes the lining to thicken, and progesterone, which maintains the thickened lining of the uterus.

The most likely time for an egg to be fertilised is between days 15 and 22. If fertilisation takes place, the menstrual cycle stops while the fertilised egg develops in the uterus.

Exercise 2

1 How long does the menstrual cycle shown in the diagram last for?

2 a What happens between days 7 and 10 of the menstrual cycle?

b Where does this take place?

3 Between which days is an egg released from an ovary?

4 Describe what is happening between days 16 and 20 of the cycle.

5 a What happens during menstruation?

b Explain why this happens.

Tactics

Girls are born with thousands of unripened eggs. One egg develops each month and is released from an ovary.

Fertilisation

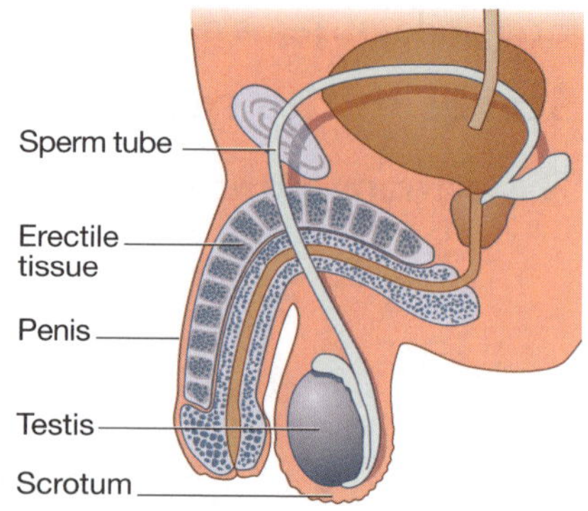

The diagram shows the main parts of the male reproductive system.

During sexual intercourse:

- the erectile tissue becomes filled with blood, causing the penis to swell and become erect
- the penis is inserted into the vagina
- sperm from the testes flows through the sperm tube and out through the end of the penis
- the sperm are normally released at the cervix, the entrance to the uterus.

The sperm swim through the uterus and along the fallopian tubes. If they meet an egg in the fallopian tubes, fertilisation may take place.

> Fertilisation is the joining together, or fusion, of a male sex cell (sperm) and a female sex cell (ovum or egg).

When an egg is fertilised, one sperm enters the egg, and the nuclei of the two cells join together. This single cell is the beginning of a new human being. Its nucleus contains information from both the mother and the father.

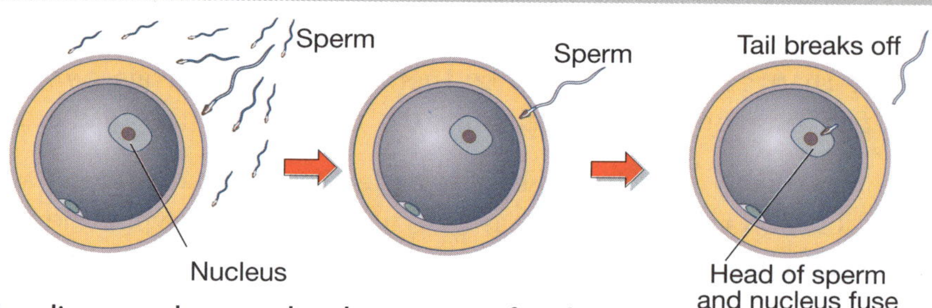

The diagram shows what happens in fertilisation.

Exercise 1

1. Which organs produce sperm?
2. During intercourse, where are the sperm normally released?
3. Explain why the penis needs to fill with blood for intercourse to take place.
4. Describe what happens in fertilisation.
5. How many new cells are made when a sperm cell and an egg cell fuse?

Tactics

Fertilisation occurs in both plants and animals when a male sex cell fuses with a female sex cell.

ED ALERT

Food and waste materials pass along the umbilical cord. They are transferred between the blood of the fetus and the blood of the mother through the placenta.

RE

From embryo to fetus

The single cell divides and these cells divide several times as they travel along the fallopian tube to the uterus. Now it is an embryo.

The developing fetus

The embryo travels to the uterus and beds itself in the lining. Here the embryo develops into a fetus. The embryo becomes a fetus when it has recognisable human features.

The fetus:

- is joined to the placenta by the umbilical cord; food, oxygen and waste materials pass along the cord
- is surrounded by a watery liquid that keeps it warm and protects it from shock.

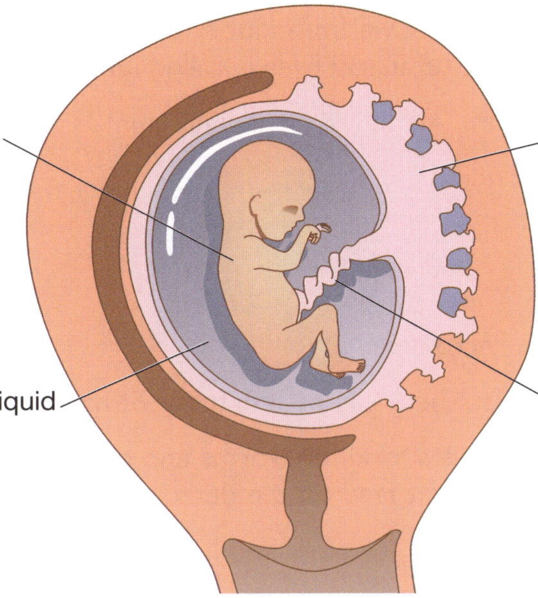

It is important to remember that the blood of the fetus and that of the mother never mix.

After nine months of pregnancy, the baby is born through the vagina. A human baby is helpless at birth and relies on care from the parents if it is to survive.

Some animals produce offspring that do not need a great deal of care from their parents. A classic example is the frog. Frogs do not take care of eggs and tadpoles.

Exercise 2

1 How does the embryo reach the uterus?

2 Describe the difference between an embryo and a fetus.

3 State two reasons why the embryo is surrounded by a watery liquid.

4 What materials pass along the umbilical cord?

5 Explain the purpose of the placenta.

Tactics

It is important to remember that the blood of the fetus never mixes with that of the mother. Mother and fetus may have different blood groups and bacteria could be passed over if blood was shared.

Habitats

For much of the year, we live indoors. Most plants and animals live outdoors. The region where a particular plant or animal lives is called its habitat.

A habitat is a community of plants and animals that depend on each other.

A habitat provides:

- food
- shelter
- a place to reproduce.

In a large garden there can be a number of habitats.

- A hedge provides food for worms and other soil-based animals that feed on the dead leaves.
- It provides shelter for birds and hedgehogs.
- The birds and hedgehogs eat the animals that feed off the hedge.
- Other habitats could include a tree or a pond, or an area of bushes or flowers.

Exercise 1

1 What is a habitat?

2 State three things that a habitat must provide.

3 Explain how a hedge provides a habitat for worms.

4 Explain how a woodland habitat provides food for a fox.

5 A garden pond provides space for fish to reproduce. What else should live in the pond to make it a suitable habitat for fish?

Tactics

Remember that the three things a habitat must provide are food, shelter and a place to reproduce.

RED ALERT A habitat supports a variety of plants and animals that depend on each other. **RED**

How plants and animals are adapted

The animals in any habitat have special features that enable them to live there.

Fish can live in a pond but a fox cannot. To live in a pond a fish needs:

- fins so that it can move through the water
- a tail so that it can control its direction of movement
- gills for gas exchange
- a streamlined shape.

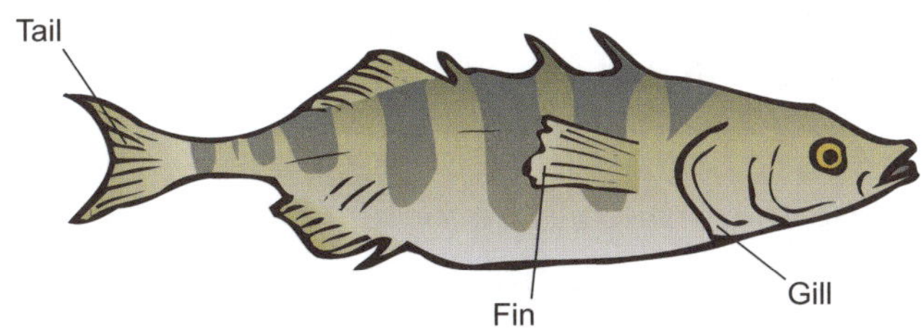

These adaptations are important for a fish to survive.

To live in the wild a fox needs:

- strong hind legs so that it can run fast to catch its prey
- canine teeth to tear flesh when it feeds
- lungs for gas exchange.

Plants are also adapted with special features that suit their habitat. Woodland plants often develop and flower in the spring when light can penetrate through the trees. In summer, when there is little light due to leaves being fully opened, they are dormant.

The plants in a pond grow most vigorously in summer when there is the greatest amount of sunlight, which gives them energy for making food and growth. They are adapted to absorb energy from the Sun by floating on the water or having long stems so that their leaves are close to the water surface.

Exercise 2

1 State four ways in which a fish is adapted to live in water.

2 State three ways in which a fox is adapted to live on land.

3 Bluebells are woodland plants. Explain why they grow and flower in spring.

4 State two ways in which plants that grow in ponds are adapted to absorb energy from the Sun.

Tactics

In tests you may be provided with a diagram of an animal and asked how it is adapted to survive in its habitat. Look at the features of the animal and try to explain why these are necessary for movement, feeding and reproduction.

Feeding

The key difference between plants and animals is that plants make their own food.

Plants use carbon dioxide from the air and water from the soil to manufacture food in the form of glucose, a simple sugar.

- Because they make all the food for the animals in a food chain, plants are called producers.
- Animals such as worms that feed directly off plant material are called primary consumers.
- Secondary consumers feed off primary consumers.
- Tertiary consumers feed off secondary consumers.

Food webs

Some animals, called herbivores, feed off plants. Some animals, called carnivores, feed off other animals. There are also animals, such as humans, that feed off both plants and other animals. These animals are called omnivores.

> The feeding relationships in a habitat are shown by a food web, which consists of a number of food chains.

The diagram shows a food web based on an oak tree as the producer.

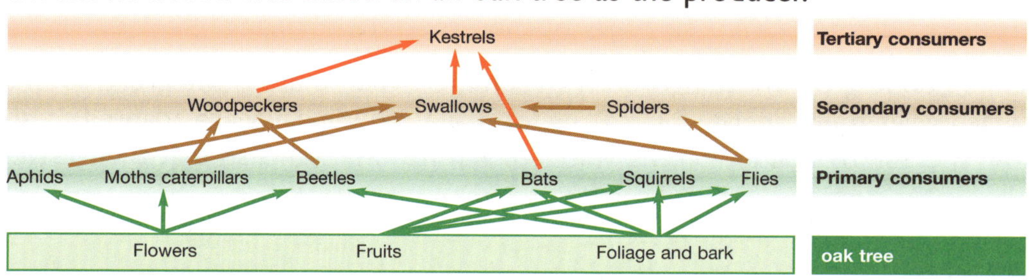

Exercise 1

1 One of the food chains that make up this web is:

flower → moth caterpillar → ____________ → kestrel

Write down the name of the animal that is missing from the food chain.

2 Describe the different ways in which plants and animals obtain their food.

3 What two substances do plants use to manufacture food?

4 Describe the differences between a herbivore, a carnivore and an omnivore.

5 In the food web shown in the diagram, what is the producer?

Tactics

The arrows on a food chain or food web show the direction of energy flow. A common error in Key Stage 3 tests is to draw the arrows in the wrong direction.

RED ALERT Remember that the arrows on a food chain or food web show the direction of energy flow. **RED**

Changes in the environment

If you observe a habitat such as a hedge or a tree in a garden, you notice that changes are continually taking place.

Each day there are changes in:

- the light intensity
- the temperature
- the moisture level.

Over the course of a year there are even greater variations in all these factors. These changes can affect:

- the number of organisms in a habitat
- the type of organisms in a habitat
- the activity of the organisms in a habitat.

Tree covered in leaves

Same tree – leafless

Lots of aphids live on the leaves of this tree in summer

Few aphids survive the winter

Survival

To survive in a changing habitat, organisms need to adapt to cope with the extreme conditions. The tree loses its leaves in winter to reduce the loss of heat and water – it may not be able to take in water if the ground is frozen.

> Insects burrow into the ground or leaf litter, and their offspring survive the winter as eggs.
>
> Large animals such as squirrels build up a store of food to help them to survive.

Exercise 2

1. Describe how the light intensity and temperature change in a garden habitat from early to late summer.
2. Explain why changes in the moisture level in a garden habitat vary from season to season.
3. State two reasons why some trees lose their leaves in winter.
4. How do insects survive cold winters?
5. Suggest why ladybirds are more active in summer than in winter.

Tactics

Some trees are adapted to keep their leaves in winter. The leaves are in the shape of needles. They have a small surface area to minimise water loss.

Different organisms

Human beings are a species, which is a type of organism. Most human beings:

- have a head, two arms and two legs
- walk on two legs
- reproduce sexually
- breathe with their lungs.

The list is endless, but what about the ways in which human beings differ? Here are some obvious ones:

- height
- weight
- colour of hair or skin or eyes.

Again, the list is endless.

> Differences between species and between individuals of a species is called variation.

Genetics

What determines whether you are a human being, rather than a fly or a cat or a rabbit? The answer is the genetic information from your parents. This information was contained in the sperm and the egg that joined at the instant you were created. The same information is contained in the nuclei of most of your body cells. This information determines the natural colour of your hair, your sex (whether you are male or female) and the colour of your eyes.

Exercise 1

1. Which of the four characteristics of humans given above are common to dogs?
2. What name is given to differences between different humans?
3. Where does an individual's genetic information come from?
4. Explain why the genetic information carried in the cells of an individual is identical in every cell.
5. Explain whether an individual's hair colour is always determined by genetic information inherited from its parents.

Tactics

Remember that variation describes the differences both within a species and between different species.

RED ALERT Genetic information is inherited equally from the mother and the father.

Nature or nurture

The genetic information that you inherit influences a number of other things, such as:

- how tall you are
- your body shape
- your weight.

Genetics is not the only factor that determines your height, shape and weight. These are also influenced by environmental factors such as:

- your diet – whether you eat a balanced diet or a lot of fatty foods and chocolate
- exercise – whether you walk or cycle to school or travel in a car
- physical activity – whether you take an active part in sport or prefer to watch television.

There are some aspects of your physical appearance that are nothing to do with genetics – they are totally controlled by environmental factors. These include:

- the length of your hair
- whether you wear an earring
- the length of your finger nails.

Most of the differences between human beings are due to a combination of genetic and environmental factors – nature and nurture.

Exercise 2

1 State three environmental factors that can affect an individual's body weight.

2 Decide whether each of these characteristics is determined by genetic factors, environmental factors, or both:

  a body weight

  b hair length

  c eye colour

  d whether the hair is straight or curly.

3 Explain whether skin colour is determined by genetic factors, environmental factors, or both.

Tactics

Remember that very few characteristics are purely genetic or purely environmental.

Classification

There are more than one million known species of organisms in the world, and new ones are being discovered every day. So that they know where each species fits into the pattern of life, scientists classify species of organisms into groups.

There are four kingdoms or groups of organisms that are similar in their behaviour:

- plants – these have many cells and make their own food
- animals – these have many cells. They eat other organisms and have senses, nerves and muscles
- fungi – such as mushrooms. These organisms do not have a cellular structure. Instead, they are made up of threads of material. They digest their food outside the body before absorbing the products
- protists – single-celled organisms that can make their own food (like plants) or feed from their surroundings (like animals).

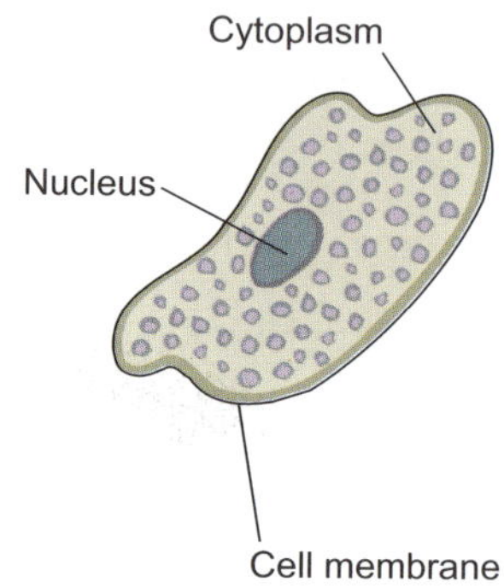

An amoeba

The diagram shows an amoeba. This is a single-celled organism in the protist kingdom. Amoebas can live in ponds and wet ground. They can also live in animals such as humans. They reproduce by dividing into two.

> *Organisms are grouped within each kingdom according to their lifestyle and appearance.*

Exercise 1

1 Which kingdom of organisms can make their own food?

2 Which kingdom consists of single-celled organisms?

3 In what way are fungi different from the species in the other three kingdoms?

4 Explain whether an amoeba reproduces sexually or asexually.

5 Explain why scientists classify species into different kingdoms.

Tactics

You need to be able to classify a species according to its characteristics.

ED ALERT Learn the characteristics of each group of vertebrates. RED A

Classes of animals

Animals are classified as vertebrates (animals with backbones) or invertebrates (animals without backbones). The different groups of vertebrates and invertebrates are shown in the diagram.

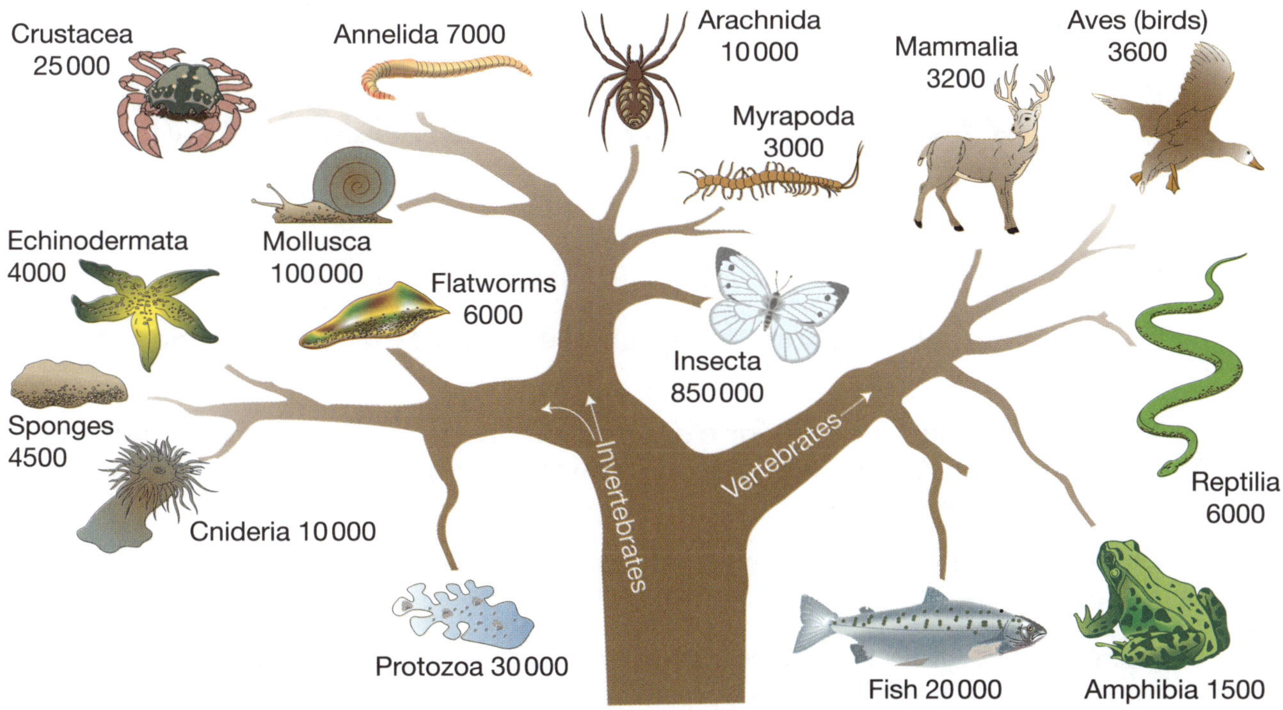

The numbers by each group give the approximate number of known species.

Exercise 2

1 What is the difference between vertebrates and invertebrates?

2 State three differences between fish and reptiles.

3 To which group of invertebrates do snails belong?

4 State one difference between species in the groups Mammalia and Aves.

5 State one similarity between species in the groups Fish and Amphibia.

Tactics

You do not need to remember the different groups of animals, but you do need to be able to group animals according to their physical appearance.

2

Surviving in the laboratory

Dangers

Imagine yourself in a room that is full of explosive gases and bottles of chemicals.

The gases are just waiting for a spark to set them off. Some of the chemicals are poisonous. Others will corrode your clothing and your skin if you come into contact with them.

This could be the scene for a bad dream or a horror movie, or it could be a science lesson!

The diagram shows some potential hazards in a school science laboratory. Make a list of those that you can see.

Safety

Despite all the hazards, there are very few accidents in school science laboratories. Some schools give pupils a list of 'dos' and 'don'ts', but the best rule is act sensibly at all times.

The diagrams show some of the everyday safety precautions that you should always take to ensure safety in the laboratory.

Always protect your eyes when handling chemicals.

Make sure the air hole is closed when lighting a bunsen burner.

Do not walk about with a lighted splint.

Strike a match by moving it away from the body.

What are acids and alkalis?

Many substances in the world around us are acids or alkalis.

- The sour taste we get when we bite into an apple is an acid.
- The sour taste we get when we taste vinegar is an acid.

Acids always have a sour taste although we would be very unwise to taste most of them!

Acids are found in lemons, oranges and limes. These are called citrus fruits and the acid is citric acid. The sourness of vinegar is caused by the acid it contains. This is called ethanoic acid.

There are three common acids we use in the laboratory. They are sometimes called mineral acids. They are:

Sulphuric acid	H_2SO_4
Nitric acid	HNO_3
Hydrochloric acid	HCl

Alkalis are in some ways the opposite of acids. They will react with and 'cancel out' acids.

Common alkalis in the home are found in bicarbonate of soda, washing powders and washing soda. Common alkalis in the laboratory include:

Sodium hydroxide	$NaOH$ (sometimes called caustic soda)
Potassium hydroxide	KOH
Calcium hydroxide	$Ca(OH)_2$
Ammonia	NH_3

Substances, such as water, that are neither acidic nor alkaline are said to be neutral.

Exercise 1

1 Write down the names of five acids.

2 Write down the names of five alkalis.

3 You are given a bottle labelled lithium hydroxide solution. Do you think it is an acid or an alkali? Why do you think this?

4 What is present in all acids? *(Hint: What does the letter H represent?)*

Tactics

Learn the names of the three common acids used in the laboratory. Students often confuse hydrochloric with hydraulic.

RED ALERT Acids and alkalis must be handled with great care. You should always wear eye protection when using them. RED

Detecting acids and alkalis

Acids and alkalis can be detected using coloured solutions called indicators.

Litmus is an indicator. If litmus is added to an acid, the solution turns red. If it is added to an alkali, the solution turns blue.

Sometimes scientists use a piece of paper soaked in litmus called litmus paper. It is easier than carrying bottles of liquid.

Acid	→	Red
Alkali	→	Blue

Universal Indicator

Litmus paper and similar indicators are useful for detecting acids and alkalis but they do not compare their different strengths. Universal Indicator is better. It is a mixture of simple indicators and it changes through a series of different colours. The pH value can be found from the colour.

The pH value is a number on a scale from 0 to 14 which shows how acidic or how alkaline a substance is. The indicator shows a different colour for different pH values.

If Universal Indicator solution turns orange when added to a substance, the pH value is 5 and the substance is a weak acid.

Scientists wanting to make a number of pH readings may use a pH meter.

	pH	Colour of Universal Indicator	Examples in the home	Examples in the laboratory
	1		car battery acid	mineral acids
STRONG ACIDS	2			
	3	red		
	4		lemon juice, vinegar	ethanoic acid
WEAK ACIDS	5	orange		
	6	yellow	soda water	carbonic acid
NEUTRAL	7	green	water, salt, ethanol	
WEAK ALKALIS	8	blue	soap, baking powder	sodium hydrogencarbonate
	9	blue-purple		
	10			ammonia solution
	11		washing soda	
STRONG ALKALIS	12	purple	oven cleaner	
	13			sodium and potassium hydroxides
	14			

The colours for a simple form of Universal Indicator.

Exercise 2

1 What colour is litmus in a neutral solution? *(Hint: Think of neutral as being halfway between acid and alkali.)*

2 Three test tubes contain different liquids. A piece of red litmus paper and a piece of blue litmus paper are added to each tube. The results are shown in the table. What can you conclude about each liquid from these tests?

Liquid	Red litmus	Blue litmus
A	Stays red	Turns red
B	Turns blue	Stays blue
C	Stays red	Stays blue

3 What is the pH value of a neutral solution?

4 What colour does Universal Indicator turn in a solution of pH value 5?

5 What pH value has a solution that turns Universal Indicator blue?

Tactics

Litmus can be used to detect acids and alkalis but it does not compare their strengths. Universal Indicator can tell the difference between an acid and an alkali.

Neutralisation

A neutralisation reaction involves an acid and a base or alkali.

When an alkali is added to an acid, the pH value changes.

In the experiment shown, sodium hydroxide solution is added slowly from a burette into 25 cm^3 of hydrochloric acid.

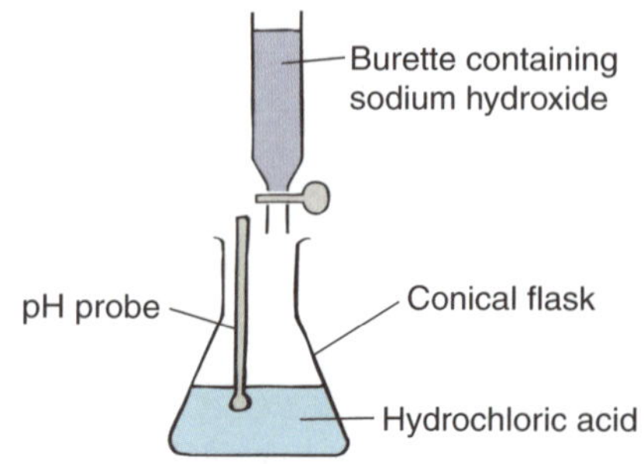

The graph shows the changes in pH during the experiment. The pH is measured using a pH probe linked to a computer.

If the correct quantities of acid and alkali are mixed together a neutral solution is formed.

The effects of the acid are cancelled out by the alkali. This change is called neutralisation.

One of the products of neutralisation is always water.

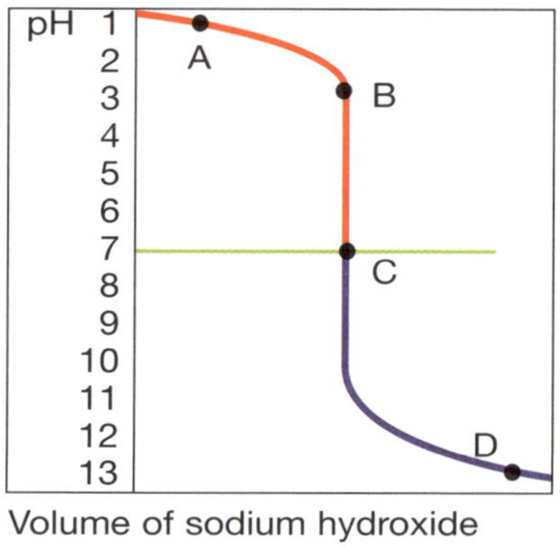

Remember:

acid + **alkali** → **salt** + **water**

You will meet this again later.

Exercise 1

1 If some sulphuric acid is spilt onto the floor, bicarbonate of soda is added. Why is this done?

2 Describe how the pH changes when sodium hydroxide is added to hydrochloric acid.

3 Look at the diagram above. At which point A, B, C or D, is the mixture:
- **a** exactly neutral?
- **b** most acidic?
- **c** most alkaline?

4 Which of the substances in this list could neutralise an alkali?
bicarbonate of soda lemon juice lime

Tactics

Remember that an acid is needed to neutralise an alkali and an alkali is needed to neutralise an acid.

Examples of neutralisation

1 **Acids in digestion**
You have several hundred cubic centimetres of hydrochloric acid in your stomach. This is used in the digestion of food. Minor problems of indigestion are caused by too much acid in the stomach. This can be neutralised by adding a weak alkali. This is called an antacid. Suitable antacids are milk of magnesia (a suspension of magnesium hydroxide) and bicarbonate of soda (sodium hydrogencarbonate).

2 **The acidity of soils**
If a farmer's soil becomes too acidic, a good yield of crops cannot be grown. Rain and artificial fertilisers make the soil more acidic. The excess acidity can be treated with lime (calcium hydroxide).

3 **Wasp and bee stings**
Wasp and bee stings are treated in different ways. A wasp sting is treated by adding vinegar (a weak acid). A bee sting is treated using bicarbonate of soda (an alkali). In both cases the remedy neutralises the sting.

4 **Removing acid gases from gases leaving power stations**
Coal-fired power stations can produce sulphur dioxide. This gas can be dangerous. It is an acidic gas. It can be removed by passing it over limestone. The limestone neutralises the acidic gas. Calcium sulphate is formed and this can be used to make plasterboard.

5 **Neutralising acidity in lakes**
Lakes can become acidic due to acidic gases in the air. This acidity can be removed by putting blocks of limestone into the lake.

Exercise 2

1 Suggest how wasp stings are different from bee stings.

2 The pain of a nettle sting can be reduced by rubbing it with a dock leaf. This contains a weak alkali. Suggest what is in a nettle sting and why the pain is reduced.

3 Inland lakes can become too acidic for fish to live in. What can be added to the lake to neutralise the water?

4 Tim wants to find which of two different brands of antacid tablet contains more alkali. He measures out 25 cm^3 samples of acid into two beakers. He drops tablets of Brand A into one beaker and tablets of Brand B into the other. He keeps doing this until the solutions stop fizzing. How could he tell which antacid, A or B, contains more alkali?

Tactics

You will find other examples of neutralisation as you go along. Remember an acid and an alkali are needed.

Making new materials

Bricks have been made for thousands of years. The method for making bricks has not changed greatly.

The diagram summarises the way bricks are made.

In stages 2–3 the mixture is soft and could be cut with a knife.

During stage 3 the bricks start to harden as they are being shaped.

In the baking a chemical change takes place and a new hard material is produced. It is impossible to turn a brick back to its original form.

A change that can be reversed is called a physical change. Salt dissolves in water to form a salt solution. The salt can be recovered in a solid form by evaporating the water away.

1. Clay, sand and coal dust are collected
2. These materials are mixed
3. Made into brick shapes
4. Left to dry for three days
5. Baked in an oven at 1200°C
6. Left to cool

Chemical change is sometimes called permanent change and physical change is called temporary change.

Exercise 1

1 Are the following changes chemical or physical?

- **a** The burning of wood
- **b** The melting of ice
- **c** Baking bread
- **d** Boiling water
- **e** Drying wet clothes

2 Here is a list of materials used to make houses:
bricks cement glass plastic roofing tiles
steel stone blocks wood
Which materials are manufactured and which exist in the environment?

Tactics

Make sure you are clear about the differences between chemical and physical changes. A chemical change produces new materials and cannot be reversed.

RED ALERT Chemical reactions can be represented by word equations. You will need to get used to using them.

Making new materials from acids

Acids can be used to make new materials. These include two very different gases, hydrogen and carbon dioxide. The gas produced depends upon the material used to react with the acid.

Using metals

Many metals will react with dilute acids to produce hydrogen gas.

If a piece of magnesium metal is added to dilute hydrochloric acid, bubbles of colourless hydrogen gas are seen. This reaction can be summarised in a word equation as:

magnesium + hydrochloric acid → magnesium chloride + hydrogen

If a lighted splint is held close to the mouth of the test tube, the hydrogen gas burns with a squeaky pop.

Using carbonate (e.g. limestone)

A carbonate reacts with a dilute acid to form carbon dioxide gas.

If some calcium carbonate is added to dilute hydrochloric acid, bubbles of colourless carbon dioxide gas are seen. This reaction can be summarised in a word equation as:

calcium carbonate + hydrochloric acid → calcium chloride + water + carbon dioxide

The gas is bubbled through colourless limewater solution. The solution goes cloudy white.

Exercise 2

1 Name the gas produced when:
   a an acid reacts with a carbonate rock
   b an acid reacts with a metal.

2 Here is a list of materials: carbon dioxide copper oxide hydrogen sodium carbonate zinc
   a Which metal reacts with dilute sulphuric acid to form hydrogen gas?
   b Which chemical reacts with dilute sulphuric acid to form carbon dioxide gas?
   c Which gas is tested for with a lighted splint?
   d Which gas is tested for with limewater?

3 Copy and complete these word equations:
   a iron + ____________________ → iron chloride + ____________________
   b sodium carbonate + hydrochloric acid → ____________________ + ____________________ + ____________________

Tactics

The two gases hydrogen and carbon dioxide are very different. Hydrogen is much lighter than air and burns. Carbon dioxide is heavier than air and puts out flames. They are both colourless gases.

Burning

Burning or combustion is a chemical reaction which releases energy. When a material burns it uses up oxygen and forms one or more oxides.

Burning a candle

A candle is burning. A beaker is put upside down over the candle.

The candle continues to burn under the beaker as it uses up the oxygen.

The candle goes out when most of the oxygen is used up.

The candle forms a number of products when it burns. These include soot (carbon), carbon dioxide and hydrogen oxide (water).

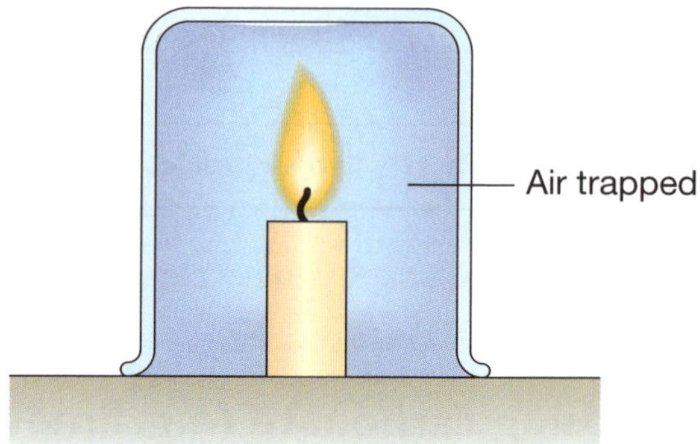

Putting fires out

The diagram shows the fire triangle. On the three sides of the triangle are fuel, air and heat. For a fire to continue to burn all three must be present.

To put out a fire one or more of these have to be removed.

A fire of paper or cardboard can be put out by spraying water. The water lowers the temperature (removes heat). The fire goes out.

Exercise 1

1 Which gas in the air is used up when a candle burns?

2 Why does a candle continue to burn longer under a 1000 cm^3 beaker than under a 250 cm^3 beaker?

3 A chip pan fire should be put out by covering the pan with a wet cloth. What side of the fire triangle is being removed?

4 In a forest fire aeroplanes drop water onto the fire and workers on the ground cut down all of the trees in the path of the fire. What does each of these remove?

Tactics

Remember burning requires a fuel, oxygen (or air) and a source of heat.

Substances that burn

Some substances burn and others do not. A substance that burns, e.g. wood, is said to be combustible.

A substance that catches alight easily is said to be flammable.

Substances that are flammable sometimes have a hazard warning sign on them.

Metals that burn

Some metals burn to form a metal oxide.

When magnesium is heated in air, the magnesium burns with a bright white flame.

The white ash formed is called magnesium oxide.

The reaction can be summarised as:

magnesium + oxygen → magnesium oxide

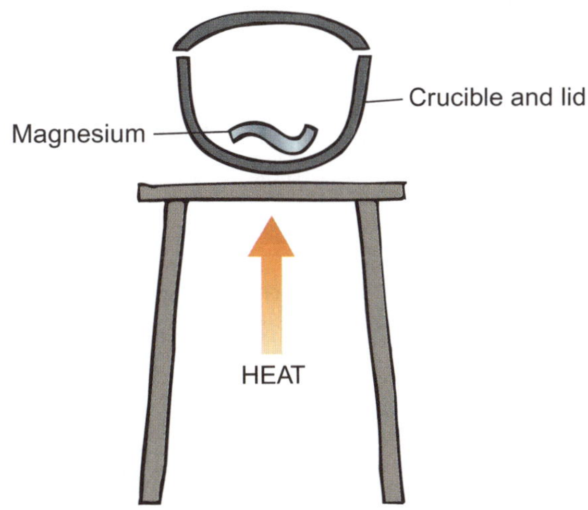

Exercise 2

1 Here are a list of materials. The ones that are combustible could be used on a bonfire.

Which ones could be used on a bonfire?

bricks cardboard newspaper scrap iron tree branches

2 Why must petrol stations be strictly no smoking areas?

3 What is formed when the metal zinc is burned?

4 When the magnesium is heated in the crucible, the lid has to be lifted from time to time. Why is this?

Tactics

Some metals burn to form metal oxides. You will know, however, that many do not. This depends on the reactivity of the metal.

Solids, liquids and gases

Materials can be classified into three possible states: solids, liquids or gases.

Water for example can exist as ice (a solid) below 0°C, water (a liquid) between 0°C and 100°C and steam (a gas) above 100°C.

> The temperature at which a solid turns to a liquid is called the melting point. At the same temperature a liquid turns to a solid.
>
> The temperature at which a liquid turns to a gas is called the boiling point.

Changes of state
The diagram shows how the three states of matter can be changed.

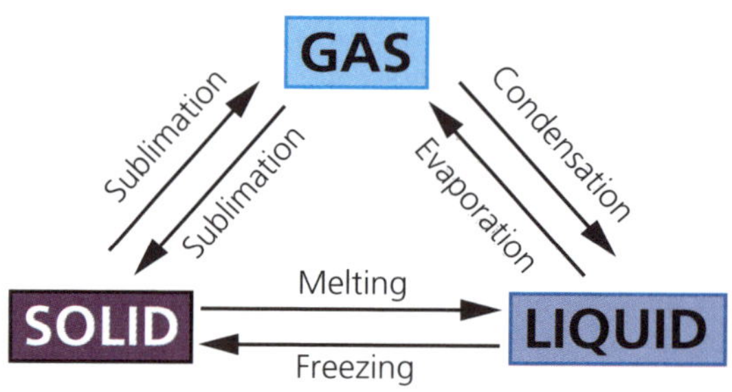

Exercise 1

1 What is the melting point of ice?

2 What is the boiling point of water?

Sulphur has a melting point of 114°C and a boiling point of 444°C.

3 In what state is sulphur at room temperature (20°C)?

4 In what state is sulphur at 500°C?

5 Steam is cooled to form water. What name is given to this process?

Tactics

Given the melting point and boiling point of a substance you should be able to work out whether the substance is a solid, liquid or gas at room temperature (20°C).

RED ALERT Understanding particles is difficult because they cannot be seen. Using models often helps. RED A

Particle model of solids, liquids and gases

Solids, liquids and gases are made up of very tiny particles.

The diagram shows how these particles are arranged in a solid, a liquid and a gas,

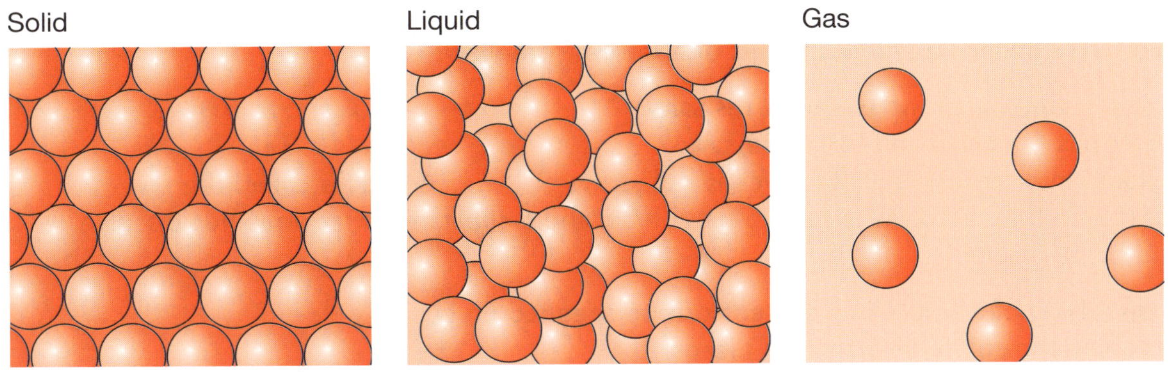

The table summarises how the particles are arranged and move in solids, liquids and gases.

State	Arrangement of particles	Movement of particles
Solid	Particles closely packed together	Little movement – only vibrations
Liquid	Particles close together but not regularly arranged	Particles have some movement
Gas	Particles widely spaced	Particles moving rapidly in all directions

Exercise 2

1 In which state are particles most widely spaced?

2 In which state are particles regularly arranged?

3 In which state are the particles moving fastest?

4 Ice floats on water. Why is this not expected? Use the table to help you.

Tactics

As you go through the course many things rely on you understanding a particle model of matter.

Solutions

Making solutions

When salt is added to water, the salt disappears from view.

The salt is still there. The water tastes salty.
The salt has dissolved and formed a salt solution.
The liquid in which the salt dissolves is called the solvent. The salt is called the solute.
A substance that dissolves is said to be soluble and a substance that does not dissolve is said to be insoluble.

The dissolving of a solute in a solvent can be speeded up by:
- crushing the solute into smaller pieces
- heating the solvent
- stirring the mixture of solute and solvent.

Saturated solution

If more and more salt is added to water, a point is reached where no more salt will dissolve.
The undissolved salt sinks to the bottom.
The solution formed contains the maximum mass of dissolved salt in a given mass of water at room temperature. It is called a saturated solution.
At room temperature a saturated solution of salt in water contains 36 g of salt in 100 g of water. Usually more solute will dissolve to form a saturated solution at a higher temperature.

Where does the solute go?

When a solution is formed the particles of the solute fit into gaps between solvent particles.

Exercise 1

1 How much salt is needed to make a saturated solution in 200 g of water at room temperature?

2 Copper sulphate crystals are blue in colour. They dissolve in water.

  a What is produced when copper sulphate dissolves in water?

  b What colour is this?

  c Which substance is the solute and which is the solvent?

3 Suggest three ways of getting copper sulphate to dissolve quicker in water.

Tactics

Make sure you understand the words solute, solvent and solution.

RED ALERT Students often confuse dissolving and reacting. If a substance dissolves it can be recovered. If it reacts, a new substance is formed and it cannot be recovered by evaporation.

Recovering a solid from a solution

Crystals of salt form when salt solution is left in a dish on a windowsill. It takes a few days. The water has evaporated away.

This process can be speeded up if the salt solution is heated.

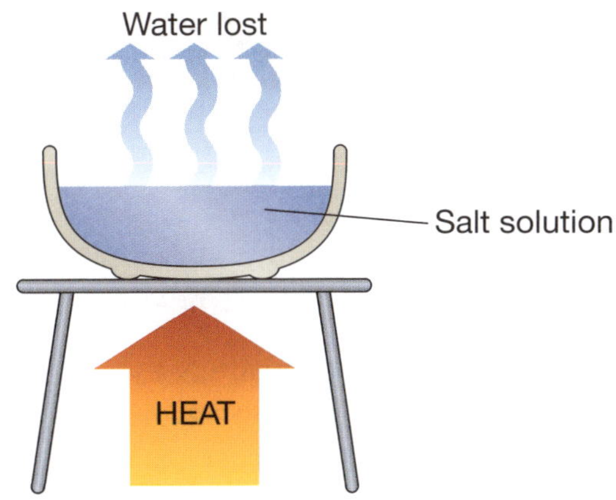

When the solution is heated the water boils and turns to steam.

Salt mining

Salt is found underground as rock salt mixed with other rocks.

It is mined by drilling a hole down to the rock salt and pumping water down to the deposits. The salt dissolves and the salt solution (called brine) is pumped up to the surface. Pure salt can be obtained by evaporating the brine.

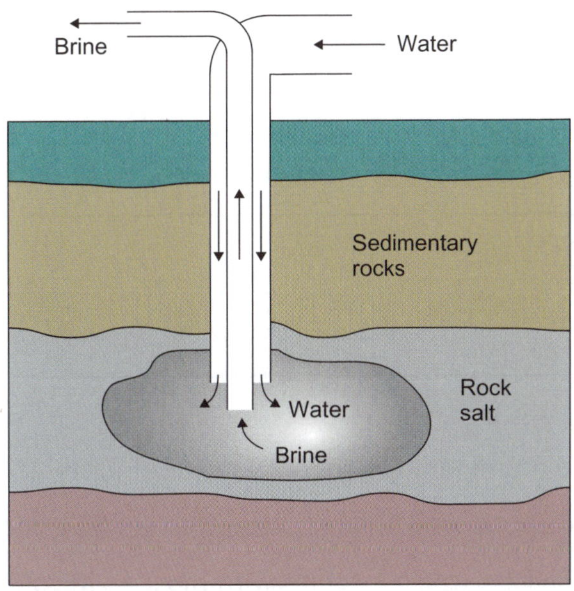

Exercise 2

1 Why do other rocks in amongst the rock salt not get mined with the salt when water is pumped down?

2 What will be formed if a saturated solution of copper sulphate is left in an open dish on a windowsill?

3 In hot countries salt is made from sea water. What is the source of energy for this process?

Tactics

It is not always wise to evaporate solutions to dryness. It can cause the solute to split up.

Solubility

The solubility of a solute in water is the maximum mass of the solute that will dissolve in 100 g of water at a particular temperature.

34 g of potassium chloride are dissolved in 100 g of hot water. The solution is then left to cool. Crystals of potassium chloride start to form below 20°C.

A saturated solution has been formed when crystals start to be seen.

> The solubility of potassium chloride in water at 20°C is 34 g per 100 g of water.
>
> Work out the maximum mass of potassium chloride that would dissolve in 10 g of water at 20°C.
>
> $$\text{Mass} = \frac{34 \times 10}{100} = 3.4\text{ g}$$

The table gives the solubility of potassium chloride at different temperatures.

Temperature in °C	10	20	30	40	50	60	70	80
Solubility in g per 100 g water	31	34	38	41	43	46	49	51

There is a pattern in these results.

As the temperature increases the solubility of potassium chloride increases.

More potassium chloride dissolves in 100 g of hot water than in cold.

A similar pattern is found with most solid solutes.

Exercise 1

1 What mass of potassium chloride would dissolve in 100 g of water at 40°C to form a saturated solution?

2 What mass of potassium chloride would dissolve in 10 g of water at 80°C to form a saturated solution?

3 23 g of potassium chloride are dissolved in 50 g of hot water. Below which temperature will crystals start to form?

4 Predict the solubility of potassium chloride in water at 25°C.

5 What would you see if a saturated solution of potassium chloride at 60°C is cooled to 20°C?

Tactics

Remember that when you quote a solubility it must refer to 100 g of solvent and a temperature.

RED ALERT If you need to find an answer from a graph, do it carefully. Give the answer the correct unit. **RED**

Solubility curves

A solubility curve is a line graph showing how the solubility of a solute changes with temperature.

On the grid there are two line graphs – one for alum and one for sodium chloride.

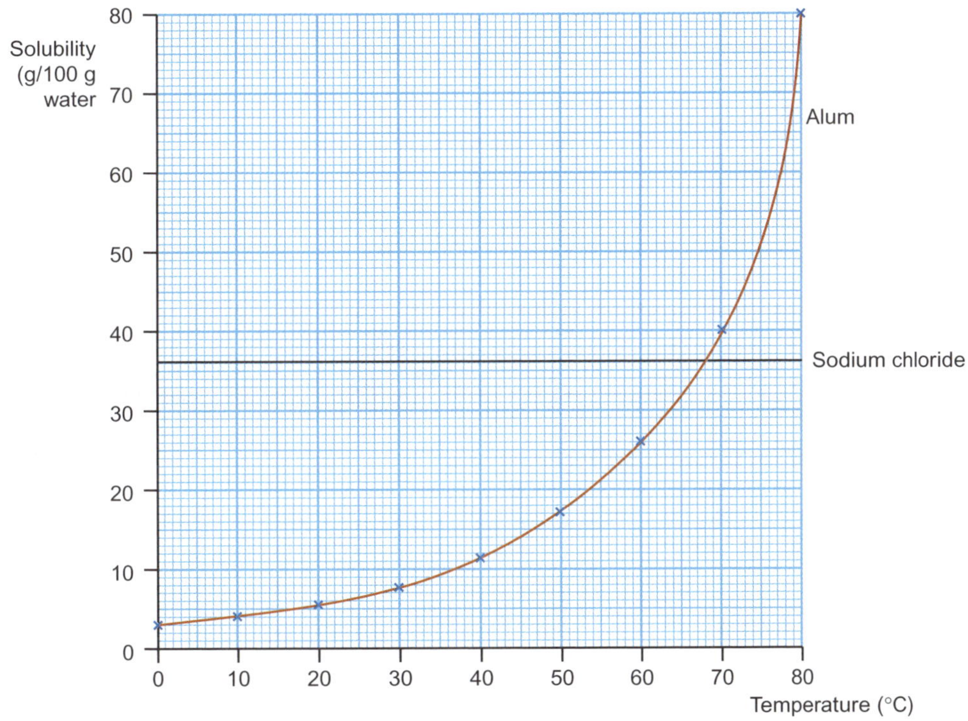

The solubility of alum increases with temperature. You could dissolve about 20 times as much alum in hot water as in cold.

The solubility of sodium chloride is about the same at all temperatures. This is unusual.

Exercise 2

1 Use the graph to help you answer these questions.
  - a What mass of alum is needed to form a saturated solution with 50 g of water at 40°C?
  - b Which solute, alum or sodium chloride, is most soluble at 20°C?
  - c Which solute, alum or sodium chloride, is most soluble at 70°C?
  - d At which temperature do alum and sodium chloride have the same solubility? *(Hint: Look at where the two graphs cross.)*

2 Draw a solubility curve for potassium chloride using the table on the previous page.

3 Sodium chloride is mined by pumping cold water down to the salt deposits to dissolve the salt and form a salt solution. Why is it no better to use hot water than cold?

Tactics

Questions involving solubility curves usually provide good opportunities to score marks.

Separating mixtures

Separating a mixture of salt and sand

If the mixture is added to water, the salt dissolves but the sand does not.

If the solution is poured through a filter, the salt solution passes through the filter paper but the sand does not.

The diagram shows how sand can be separated from the salt solution by filtering.

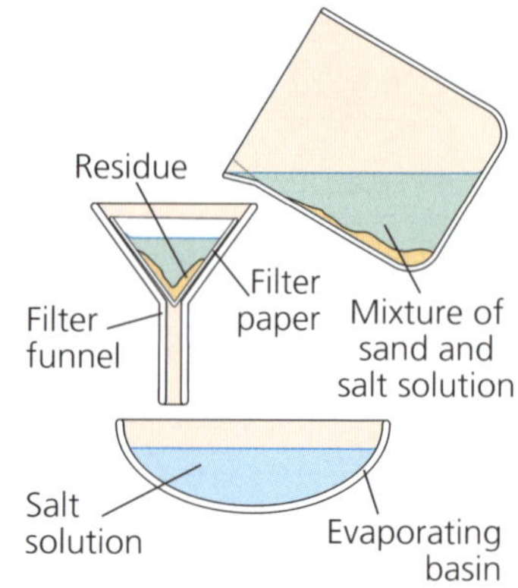

Water can be recovered from a salt solution by distillation.

Separating water from salt solution

The salt solution is heated. The water boils and escapes from the flask. The steam escapes into the condenser. Here the steam condenses and forms liquid water. This is collected in the receiver.

Distillation can be thought of as boiling followed by condensation.

The impurities, salt in this case, remain in the flask.

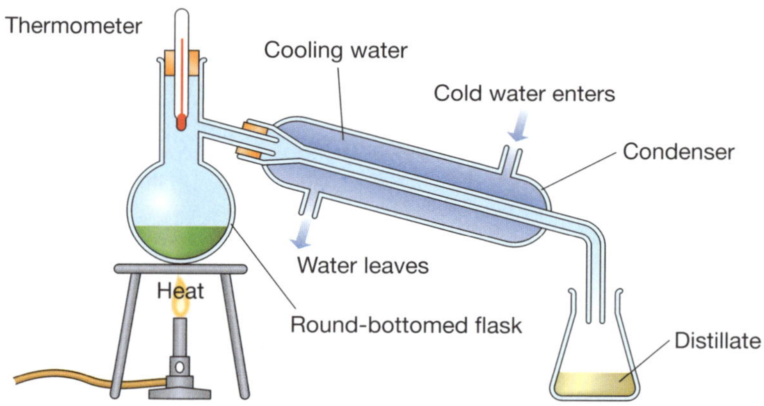

Exercise 1

1 Write a brief account of how you could get solid samples of salt and sand from a mixture of the two.

2 What is the temperature on the thermometer in the distillation apparatus during the distillation?

3 A flow of cold water passes through the condenser. What is the job of this water?

4 Why is it important that the condenser points downward?

Tactics

Make sure you can draw a labelled diagram of the distillation apparatus.

RED ALERT Filtering and distillation are important techniques. Make sure you know when each is used. RED

Separating mixtures of dyes

Mixtures of dyes dissolved in water can be separated by chromatography.

A drop of the solution containing a mixture of dissolved substances is placed at the bottom of a piece of filter paper. This is dipped into water and left. Water rises up the filter paper and the different dissolved substances separate as they move at different rates. Each different substance forms a spot on the filter paper.

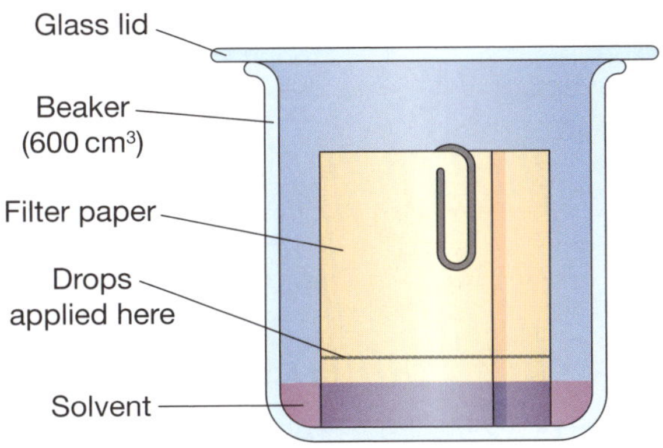

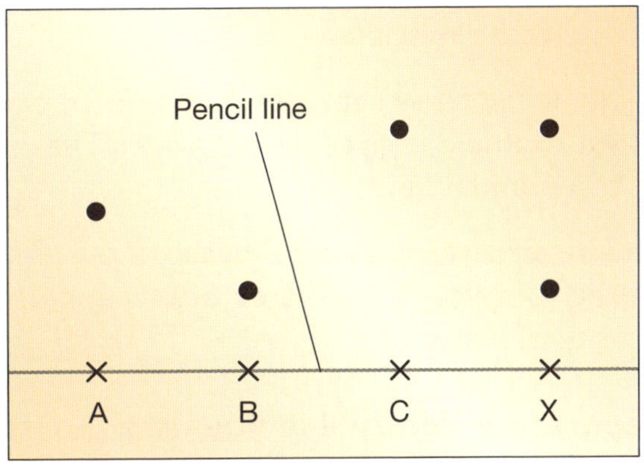

On the piece of filter paper, called a chromatogram, you can see the results obtained with three dyes: A, B and C.

There is also a mixture of dyes X. From the results it can be concluded that:

- X is a mixture of two dyes because there are two spots on the chromatogram
- X contains dye B and dye C but not dye A. X has two spots – one at the same height as dye B and one at the same height as dye C.

Chromatography is used by forensic scientists. They work with police officers to solve crime. They could use chromatography to find which pen a criminal used to write a poison pen letter.

Exercise 2

The chromatogram shows the dyes present in a sample of orange squash.

It also shows the results obtained when five pure dyes, A, B, C, D and E, are used.

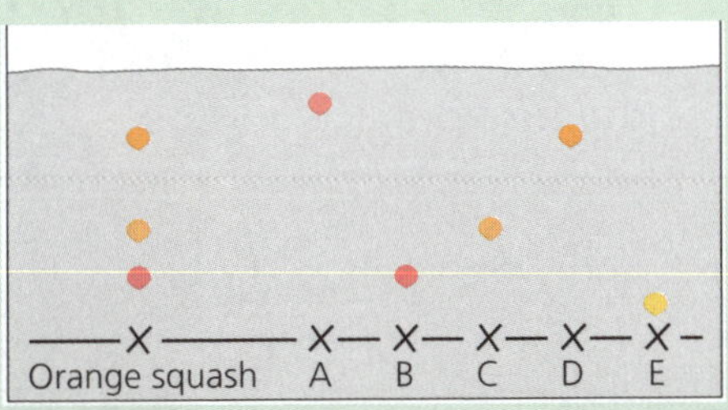

1 How do you know that the orange squash is not coloured by one pure dye?

2 How many dyes are present in the orange squash?

3 Which dyes are present in the orange squash?

4 The lines on the filter paper should be drawn in pencil and not in pen. Why is this?

Tactics

Remember chromatography is usually used to separate mixtures of coloured dyes dissolved in a solvent.

Mixing liquids

When two liquids are poured into a container:

- the liquids may mix completely together to form a single liquid. An example is ethanol and water. These liquids are said to be miscible.
- the liquids may separate out to form two different layers. An example is glycerol and water. These liquids are said to be immiscible.

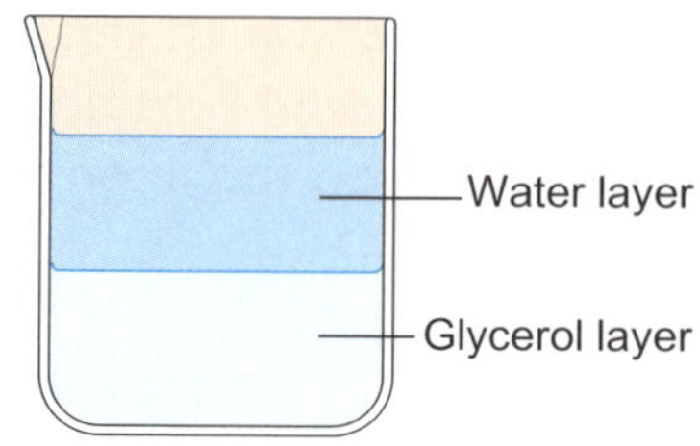

The lower layer is glycerol because the density of glycerol is greater than the density of water.

Separating immiscible liquids
The diagram shows how a mixture of glycerol and water can be separated using a separating funnel.

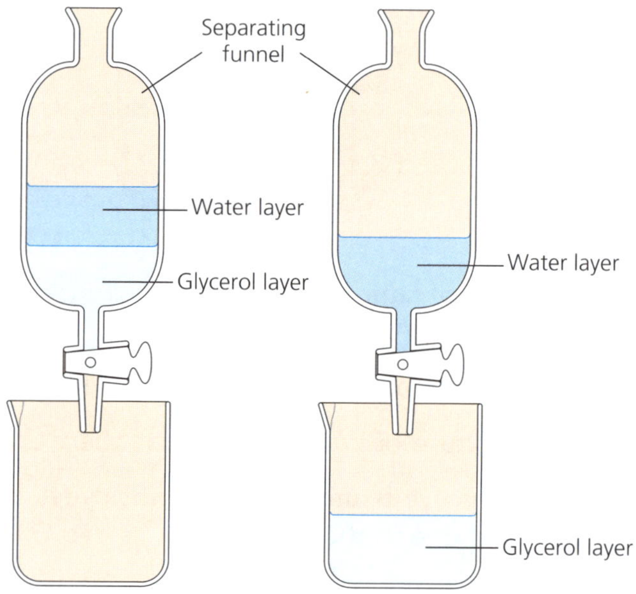

To separate the two liquids, the tap is opened until all the glycerol has run into the beaker.

The tap is then closed and the beaker is changed. The tap can be opened and the water is run into another beaker.

Exercise 1

1 The table gives the densities of three different immiscible liquids.

Liquid	Density in g/cm^3
A	1.50
B	0.80
C	1.00

a How many layers will be formed when these three liquids are poured into a beaker?

b What will be the order of the liquids from the bottom of the beaker?

2 Put the seven statements below into the correct order so they describe the method used to separate glycerol and water.

A Put a second beaker under the separating funnel.
B Put the mixture of water and glycerol into a separating funnel.
C Leave the liquids to settle out into two layers.
D Open the tap and allow the water to run into a beaker.
E Remove the stopper from the separating funnel.
F Open the tap and allow the glycerol to run into a beaker.
G Shake the separating funnel.

RED ALERT — If two miscible liquids are mixed they look the same as a pure liquid. RED A

Separating miscible liquids

Miscible liquids can be separated by fractional distillation.

When a mixture of hexane and methylbenzene are heated, hexane (boiling point 69°C) boils off before methylbenzene (boiling point 111°C).

The diagram shows the apparatus used to separate hexane and methylbenzene by fractional distillation.

- The first fraction collected up to 69°C is mainly hexane.
- The second fraction between 69°C and 111°C is a mixture of hexane and methylbenzene.
- The third fraction boiling above 111°C is mainly methylbenzene.

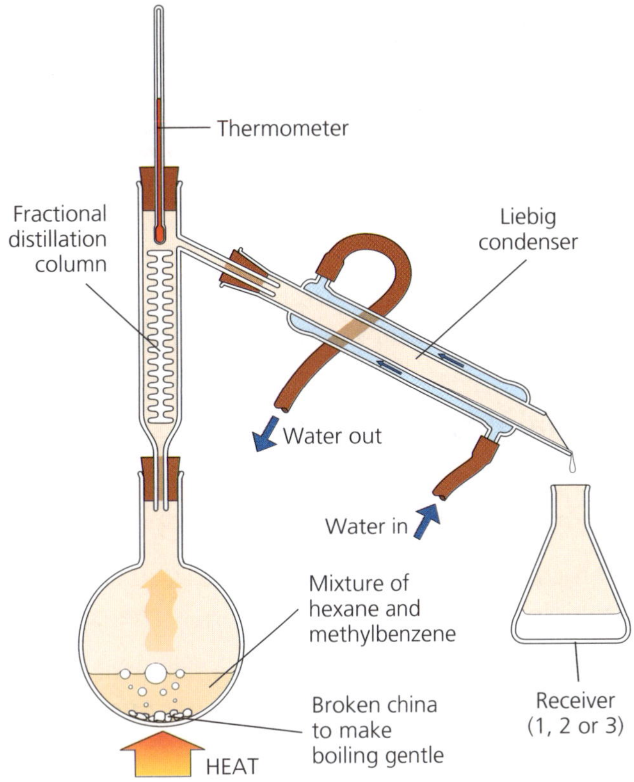

Exercise 2

1 Two miscible liquids have boiling points of 103°C and 105°C. Why is it difficult to separate them by fractional distillation?

2 Ethanol and water are two miscible liquids.

 a Which liquid is collected mainly in the first fraction?

 b Choose from the list a substance made by fractional distillation.

 beer whisky wine

Liquid	Boiling point
Water	100°C
Ethanol	78°C

Tactics

Remember that the liquids are separated in order of their boiling points. The liquid with the lowest boiling point is separated first.

Explaining with particles

Understanding that matter is made of particles will help to explain some observations you make.

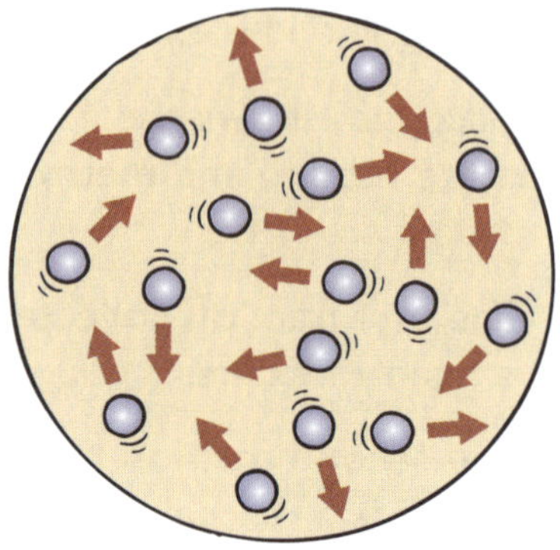

Explaining gas pressure

The particles in a gas are moving rapidly. There is no pattern to the movement. It is said to be random.

The particles hit the walls of the container. The more times the particles hit the walls, the higher is the gas pressure.

If the temperature is raised, the particles move faster so there are more collisions with the walls of the container. As a result the pressure increases.

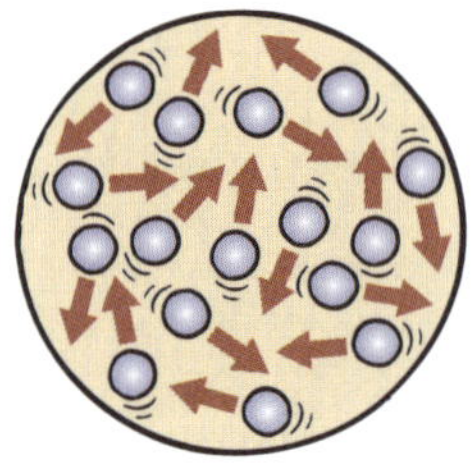

The gas is compressed into a smaller volume without changing temperature. Again, there will be more collisions with the walls. So there is an increase in pressure.

Remember: There are the same number of particles in each case.

Exercise 1

Look again at the diagram showing the particles in a gas.

1 If temperature is increased the particles move faster. Why will this lead to an increase in gas pressure?

2 More particles are put into the container (increase in concentration). Why will this lead to an increase in pressure?

3 Explain why a piece of metal expands when it is heated. Use your knowledge of particles in your answer.

Tactics

Always think about

- number of particles
- speed of movement of particles
- direction of movement of particles.

Explaining diffusion

Diffusion is the movement of particles to fill all of the available space. It occurs quickly with gases. It occurs slowly with liquids and very slowly in solids.

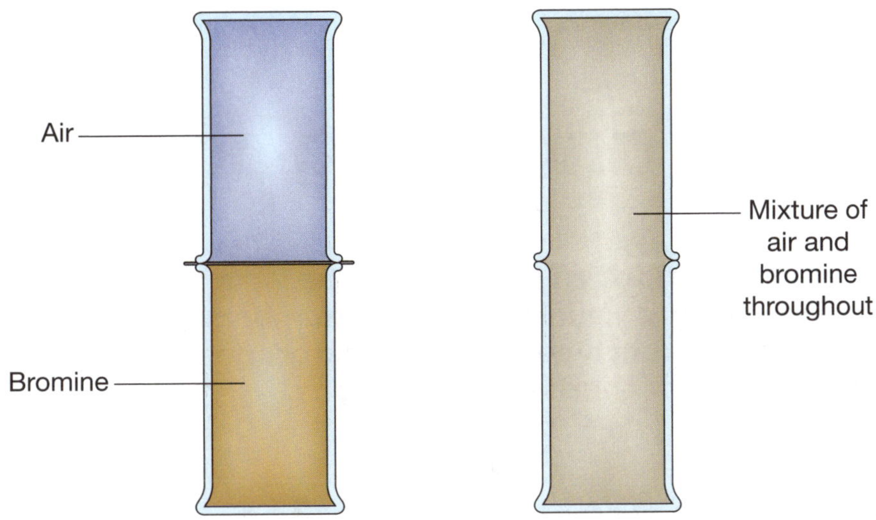

In the diagram there are two gas jars separated by a piece of card. One gas jar contains brown bromine gas and the other contains air.

When the cardboard is removed, particles move from one jar to the other. Eventually the two gas jars contain the same mixture of bromine and air.

The particles of bromine and the particles in the air mix thoroughly.

Exercise 2

A purple crystal is dropped into water in a beaker. The crystal dissolves and the purple colour spreads throughout the water. The water has not been stirred.

1 What name is given to the process taking place?

2 Why does diffusion take place faster with gases than with liquids or solids?

3 Open a bottle of perfume at the front of the room. A few minutes later the smell of perfume has spread throughout the room. The mass of the perfume and bottle have changed very little. What does this tell you about particles?

Tactics

You will meet examples of diffusion throughout your science course. Remember we always use a particle model to explain diffusion.

3

Drawing and using bar charts

Scientific information is often presented in the form of a chart or graph. These have much more visual impact than numbers given in tables. There are a number of different types of charts and graphs, but the main ones used in science are bar charts and line graphs.

When should I use a bar chart?

Bar charts are used to compare:

- the numbers of different objects, for example the numbers of different weeds growing in a lawn
- the values of a scientific quantity for different objects, for example the amount of carbohydrate contained in different foods.

Bar charts should not be used to show how changing the value of one quantity (for example the volume of water in a beaker) affects the value of another quantity (for example the time it takes to boil the water). A line graph should be used to show this.

An example

The bar chart on the opposite page compares the amount of carbohydrate in 100 g of each of a number of different foods.

When drawing a bar chart:

- the quantity goes on the vertical axis, with numbers to show the scale
- the bars are all drawn the same width
- the length of each bar shows the value of the quantity
- there is a space between each bar
- the bars can be drawn in any order.

Answer these questions about the bar chart shown below.
Check your answers with those given at the bottom of the page.

1 a Which food contains the greatest amount of carbohydrate per 100 g?

b Explain how you can tell.

2 a Which two foods shown in the chart contain equal amounts of carbohydrate?

b How much carbohydrate does 100 g of each of these foods contain?

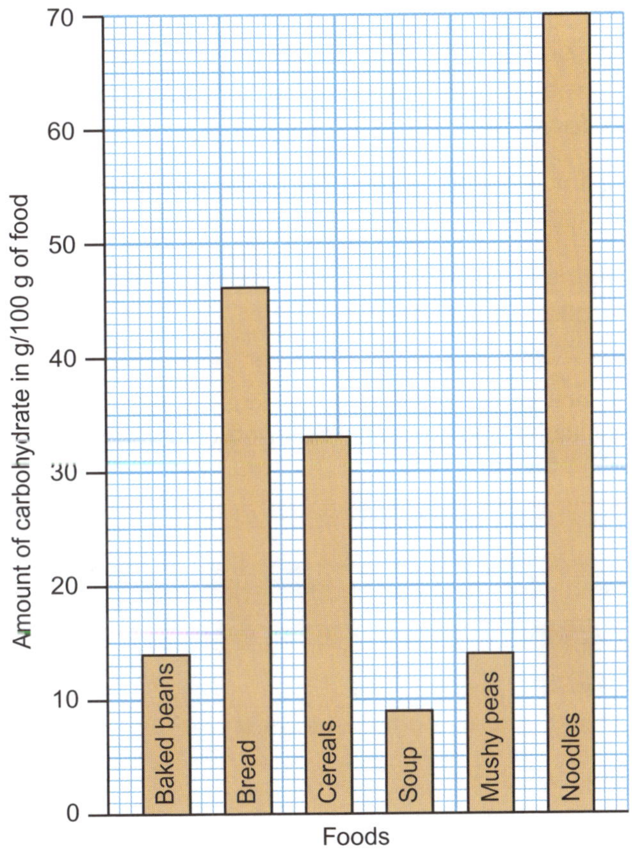

Answers

1 a Noodles

b It has the longest bar

2 a Baked beans and mushy peas

b 14 g

Where does our energy come from?

Whatever we do needs energy. Energy is needed to:

- make things move
- heat our living space
- light the areas where we live and work.

Electricity is used to produce movement in the motor of this vacuum cleaner.

Electricity provides much of the energy that we need each day.

Most of our electricity is generated by burning a fuel.

Common fuels include wood, gas, coal and oil. Of these, wood is easy to replace as more trees can be grown. Coal, oil and natural gas are fossil fuels – they took millions of years to form and cannot be replaced.

Coal was formed from giant fern-like plants that trapped energy from the Sun as they grew.

Oil and natural gas formed from animals rather than plants. When animals that lived in the sea died, their remains formed layers on the seabed. The combined effects of pressure and heat over millions of years resulted in oil and gas.

Coal, oil and natural gas are called fossil fuels because they were formed from the fossilised remains of plants and animals. They are non-renewable fuels; supplies cannot be replenished during the lifetime of the Earth.

Exercise 1

1 Write down three things that we need energy for.
2 Write down the names of three fossil fuels.
3 Which fossil fuel formed from plants?
4 Which fossil fuels formed from animals?
5 Which fuel can be replaced?

Tactics

Fossil fuels are non-renewable. This means that they cannot be replaced.

RED ALERT Remember that all the energy stored in coal, oil and natural gas originally came from the Sun.

How long will coal and oil last?

Fossil fuels are being used up rapidly:

- the UK has enough coal to last for two hundred years
- the known reserves of gas and oil will not last as long as coal
- our use of gas, oil and coal needs to be as efficient as possible
- we need to find alternative sources of energy for transport and for generating electricity.

Measuring energy

When a gas or electricity bill arrives at home, the cost is for the energy transferred through the gas pipes or electricity cables.

One joule of energy is a very small amount. It is the amount of energy that leaves your body when you lift a 1 kg bag of sugar through a height of 0.1 metre.

Energy is measured in joules (J).

To boil a kettle of water from cold needs about 600 000 J of energy, so you can imagine that a lot of energy is needed to heat enough water to fill a bath.

Exercise 2

1. Why must the use of fossil fuels be as efficient as possible?
2. What do gas and electricity bills show the cost of?
3. What is the unit of energy?
4. How much energy does it take to lift a 25 kg sack of potatoes through a height of 2 m?

Tactics

Always give the correct unit when writing down an amount of energy.

Renewable resources

A renewable energy resource is one that will not run out during the lifetime of the Earth.

Plants are renewable energy resources. They are renewable because we can grow fresh crops each year. Energy from plants is known as biomass. Other renewable resources include:

- wind
- moving water
- geothermal energy.
- waves and tides
- the Sun

Moving air and water

Energy from the Sun makes the wind blow. The energy in moving air can be used to turn wind turbines and generate electricity. These can be built singly or in groups, called wind farms.

The sea provides two important energy resources: waves and tides. Waves are caused by the wind, and tides are due mainly to the effect of the Moon pulling on the oceans.

Energy from tides is reliable, as it depends only on the Moon going round the Earth.

Electricity generated from moving water in fast-flowing rivers and streams is called hydroelectricity. Its energy source is the Sun, which causes the evaporation of water from the sea.

Exercise 1

1 What is a renewable resource?

2 What causes waves?

3 What causes tides?

4 Why are plants an important source of energy?

5 What word describes electricity generated from moving water?

Tactics

Learn the difference between a renewable and a non-renewable energy resource.

RED ALERT Do not describe a renewable resource as one that can be used over and over again. Wood can only be burned once!

Solar energy

Energy from the Sun is used directly in three different ways:

- it is used to grow crops
- it can be used to heat water
- it can be used to generate electricity.

In some countries, hot-water tanks on the roofs of houses are a common sight. Energy from the Sun is used to heat water as it passes through copper pipes.

This telephone is powered by solar cells

Solar cells use energy from the Sun to produce electricity. They are expensive to make and they only produce electricity in daylight. They are useful to power calculators, which only use a small amount of electricity.

Satellites and spacecraft use vast panels of solar cells to generate enough electricity for the on-board computers and other devices. They store surplus energy in batteries so that they have a reserve supply.

Geothermal energy is the energy in hot rocks below the Earth's surface. The energy in the rocks is used to heat water. If the rocks are hot enough, they can be used to generate steam to drive a turbine and produce electricity.

Where geothermal energy is readily available in hot rocks close to the Earth's surface, heat from the rocks can be used to heat houses, hospitals and offices. Unfortunately, there are no suitable sources of geothermal energy in the UK.

Exercise 2

1 Explain why very few houses in the UK use energy directly from the Sun to provide their hot water.

2 Write down two disadvantages of using solar cells to generate electricity.

3 How do spacecraft store the energy from solar cells?

4 What type of energy is stored in hot rocks?

5 State one advantage of using solar cells to power a calculator.

Tactics

Most renewable energy resources obtain their energy from the Sun. Tides and geothermal energy are the exceptions.

Current in circuits

To light a lamp using a cell or a low voltage power pack, there needs to be a complete route from the cell to the lamp and back again. This route is called a circuit.

In a circuit there is a complete current path from the positive terminal of the battery (a number of cells joined together) or power supply to the negative terminal.

If there is a break in the circuit, the lamp goes out. A circuit with a break in it can be used to test which materials are conductors and which are insulators.

A gap in a circuit can be used as a switch.

- If the gap is closed using a conducting material, the circuit is switched on.
- When the gap is open, the circuit is switched off.

The diagram uses circuit symbols to show a lamp that can be switched on and off.

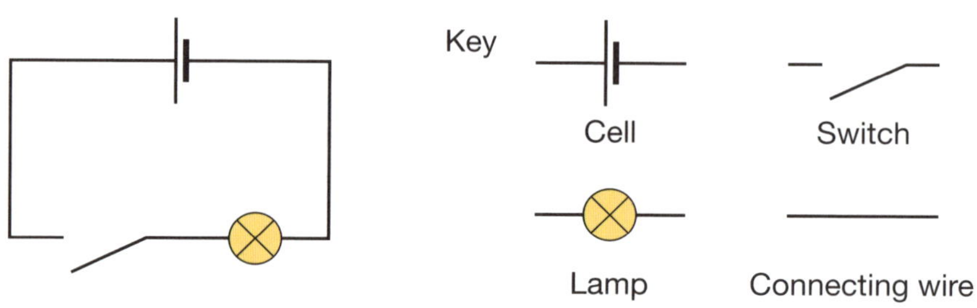

Exercise 1

1 What is meant by an electric circuit?

2 How many complete current paths are needed to light a torch lamp from a single cell?

3 Look at the diagram above. How many wires are needed to make the circuit?

4 Draw the circuit symbols for:

   a a lamp

   b a cell

   c a switch.

5 Which of these materials are conductors, and which are insulators?
aluminium brass copper Perspex polythene steel

Tactics

Remember that metals are conductors of electricity and that non-metals (except carbon) are electrical insulators.

RED ALERT

An open circuit is switched off.
A closed circuit is switched on.

RED ALERT

Different types of circuit

There are two different ways of connecting two lamps to one cell or power supply:

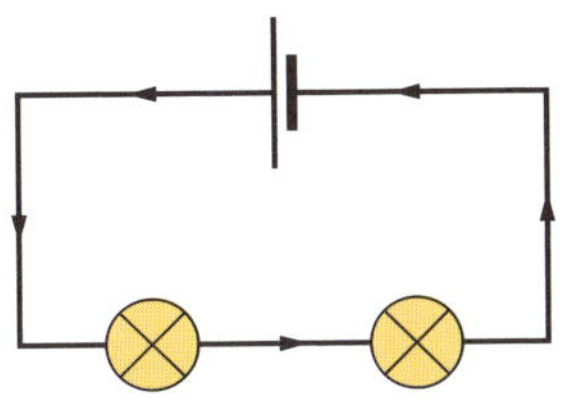

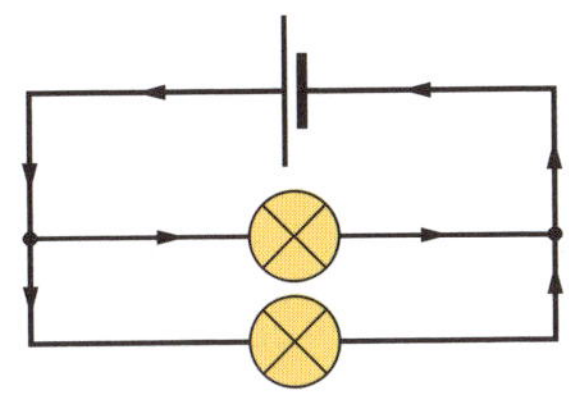

- The circuit on the left is called a series circuit. In a series circuit the current from the cell passes through each lamp in turn, one after the other.
- A parallel circuit is shown on the right. In a parallel circuit the current splits at the junction before the lamps and rejoins at the junction after the lamps.

Electronic systems such as those in computers, radios and televisions contain many series circuits but most household mains appliances are in a parallel circuit. The exception is some types of Christmas tree lights.

In a series circuit, a break anywhere in a circuit turns the whole circuit off. With a parallel circuit, switches can be put in the branches of the circuit so that each switch controls just one device.

Series control

The brightness of a lamp can be controlled by placing a variable resistor (see p. 58) in series with the lamp and the power supply. Moving the slider of the variable resistor changes the total resistance of the circuit. The greater the circuit resistance, the lower the current and the dimmer the lamp.

Exercise 2

1 Which type of circuit, series or parallel, has only one conducting path?

2 In which type of circuit does the current split and rejoin at junctions?

3 The diagrams show two different ways of connecting the lights in two bedrooms in a house.

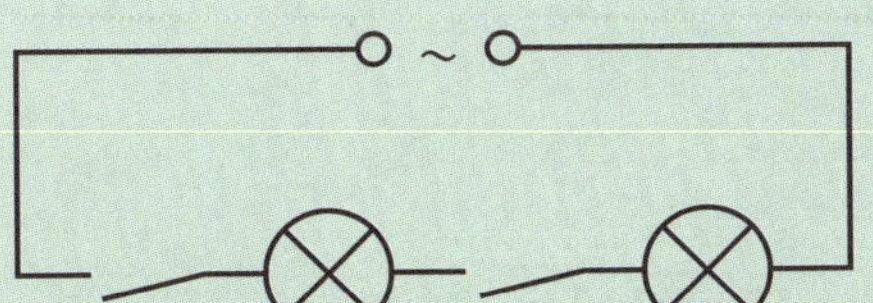

A

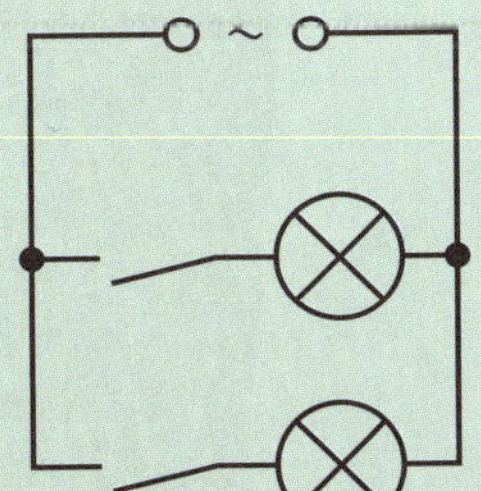

B

a Which circuit should be used?

b Explain why this circuit should be used.

Tactics

A parallel circuit allows the different components to be switched on and off without affecting the others.
In a series circuit, the components are either all switched on or all switched off.

Electric current

Measuring current

Sometimes the current passing in a circuit may be so small that it is not enough to light a lamp. Or it may be too large and would cause the lamp to 'blow'.

An ammeter:

- detects a greater range of current than a lamp does
- gives more precise measurements and enables you to make comparisons.

> An ammeter is a device that measures the size of an electric current in amperes (amps, A). Ammeters are always connected in series in a circuit.

Ammeters are either digital, which are easy to read, or analogue, which involve a needle moving over a scale. Analogue meters call for more care when taking readings, as you have to interpret the scale divisions and make judgements about readings between scale divisions.

The diagrams show how to connect an ammeter to measure the current passing into and out of a lamp.

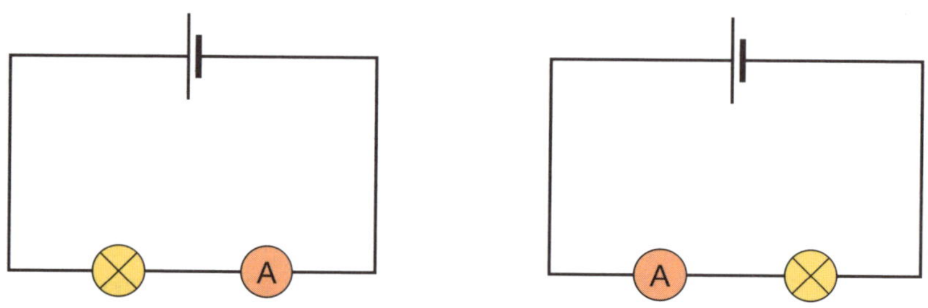

Exercise 1

1. State two reasons why a lamp filament might not light when connected in a correct circuit.
2. What device is used to measure electric current:?
3. Write down the unit of electric current.
4. Should an ammeter be connected in series or in parallel?
5. What type of meter has a pointer that moves over a scale of numbers?

Tactics

Remember that ammeters should always be connected in series with a component such as a lamp, and should never be connected directly to a power supply.

ED ALERT **Ammeters are always connected in series in a circuit.** RED A

Energy transfer

Most people are surprised to find that the current coming out of the lamp is the same as that going in. The lamp does not use up any current at all. The results obtained from the next circuit confirm this.

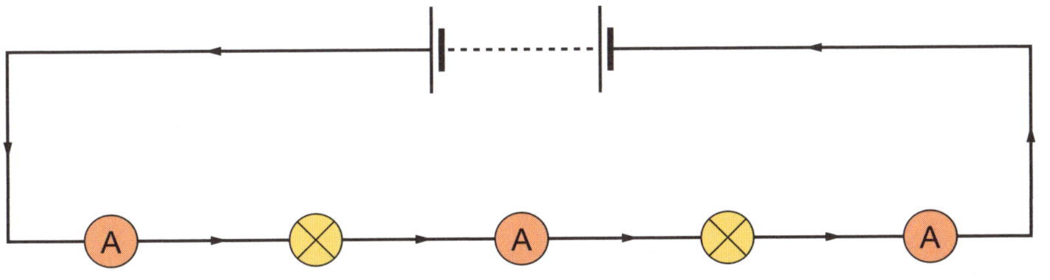

All the ammeter readings are the same; the lamps have not used any current.

The current is the same at all points in a series circuit
This may seem strange, because without a current the lamps do not work, so how do lamps produce light?

- What comes out of a lamp is energy, in the form of heat, infrared radiation and light.
- The current in a circuit transfers energy from the source, the battery or power supply, to the lamp and other components such as motors or heaters.

Energy is transferred around a circuit by moving charged particles. In metals the moving particles are electrons; these carry a negative charge. Electrons cannot move in an insulator but they are free to move around in a conductor. The electron movement is from negative to positive, even though we always mark current directions as being from positive to negative.

Exercise 2

1 A current of 2 A passes into the filament of a lamp.

 a How much current passes out of the filament?

 b How much current does the lamp use up?

2 What is the job of the current in a circuit?

3 State two types of energy emitted by a lamp that is switched on.

4 What is the direction of the current in a circuit?

Tactics

Remember that lamps, motors and other circuit components do not use up current, they transfer energy from the voltage supply.

Controlling the current

The brightness of a lamp shows the size of the electric current passing in a circuit; the brighter the lamp, the greater the current passing. The current can be made bigger or smaller if a variable resistor is included in the circuit.

A variable resistor works by changing the resistance in a circuit; the more resistance there is, the smaller the current that passes.

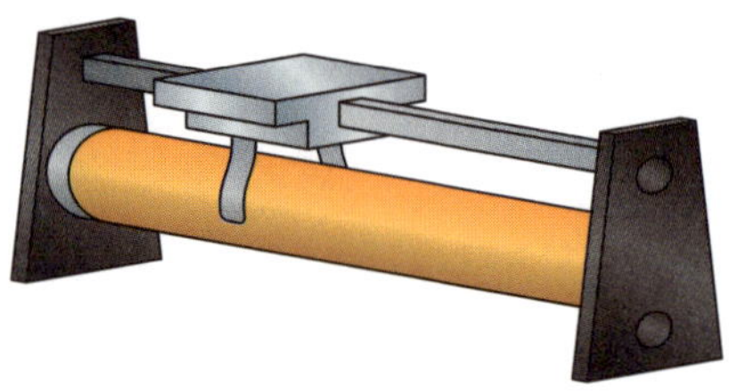

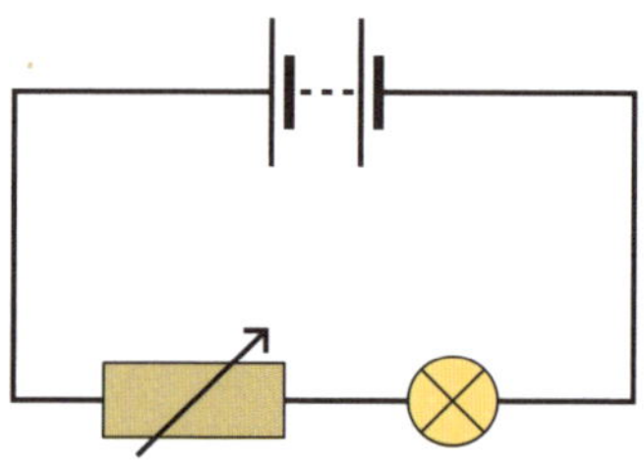

The diagram shows a common type of variable resistor and the circuit diagram shows how it is connected in a lamp-dimming circuit.

Moving the slider to one end of the variable resistor makes the lamp light at its brightest. The lamp is dimmest when the slider is moved to the opposite end.

Variable resistors can control other things besides lamps. They act as the volume control on radios and they can also be used to control the speed of an electric motor.

Exercise 1

1 When a variable resistor is used to make a lamp dimmer:

  a What happens to the resistance in the circuit?

  b What happens to the current in the circuit?

2 The diagram shows a variable resistor connected in series with a battery and a motor.

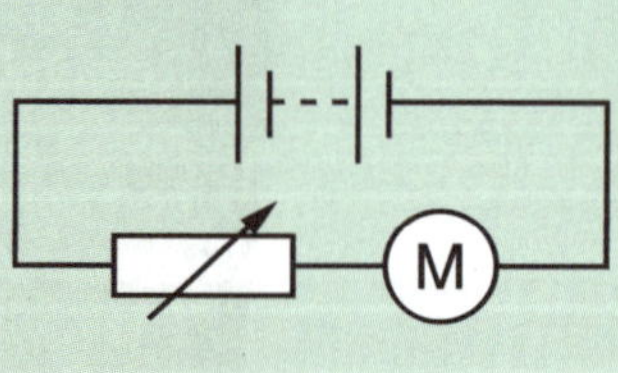

  a What type of circuit is shown, series or parallel?

  b Describe what the circuit is able to do.

Tactics

Like ammeters, variable resistors should always be connected in series.

RED ALERT

Make sure that you know the circuit symbols for common components such as cells, batteries, lamps, variable resistors and motors.

Changing the current

The size of the current that passes in a circuit depends on:

- the voltage of the current source
- the resistance of the circuit.

A variable resistor changes the current by changing the resistance. When you increase the voltage that drives the current in a circuit, the charge travels round the circuit at a greater rate, so increasing the current.

The diagram shows that when you add more lamps in a series circuit, the current becomes less because you are increasing the circuit resistance.

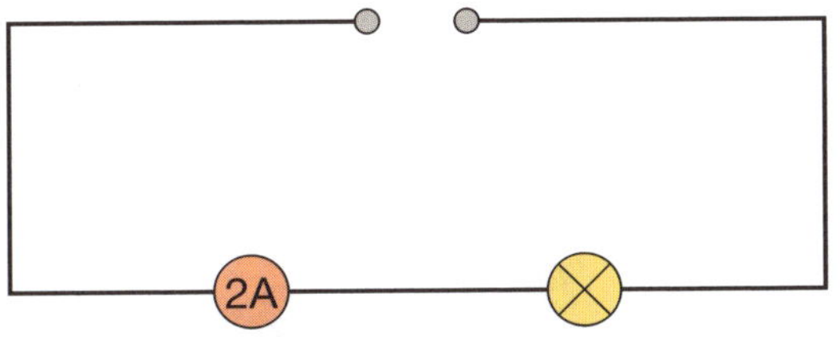

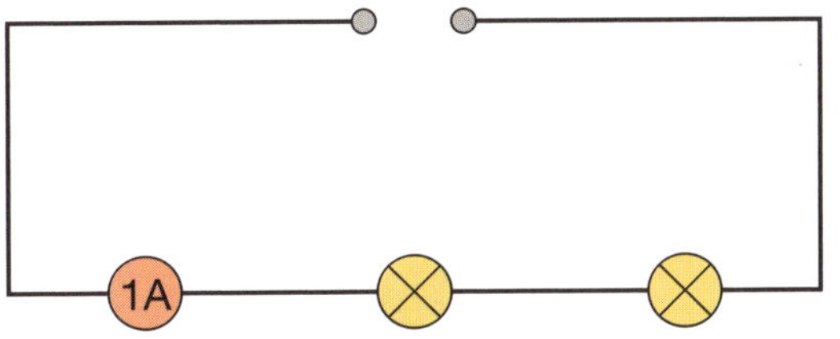

Adding more lamps in parallel causes more current in the circuit because there are more routes available for the current to pass through, as the diagram on the right shows.

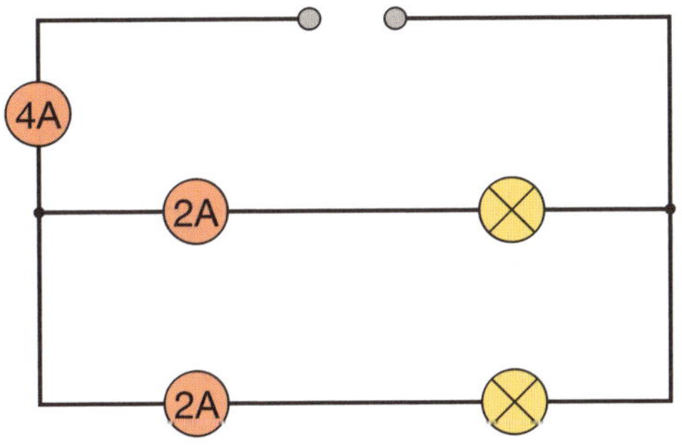

The diagram also shows that when the current splits at a junction:

- the sum of the currents along the branches is equal to the current from the power supply
- the current that passes into a junction is equal to the current that passes out.

Exercise 2

1 What happens to the current in a circuit when more lamps are added in series with the power supply?

2 What happens to the current in a circuit when more lamps are added in parallel with the power supply?

3 The diagram shows three identical lamps connected to a battery.
Write down the readings on ammeters A1, A2 and A3.

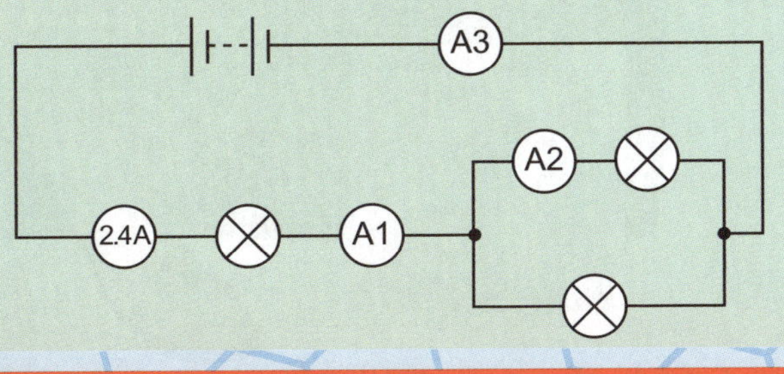

Tactics

Adding lamps in series increases the resistance of a circuit. Adding lamps in parallel decreases the resistance of a circuit.

What do forces do?

Forces are acting everywhere. No matter where you look, you will see evidence of things pushing and pulling other things.

Forces can start and stop things from moving, cause changes in direction, and change the shape of things when they squash or bend or stretch or twist them.

> Forces are described by a phrase such as object A pulls or pushes object B.

When you draw forces on a diagram, you should use an arrow to show the direction of the push or pull. Here are some examples:

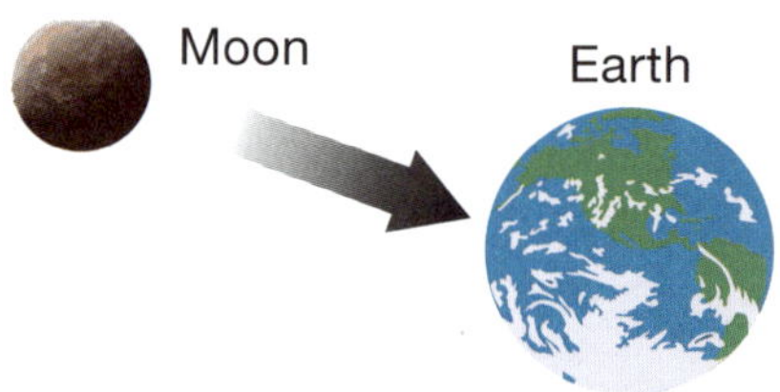

The Earth pulls the Moon.

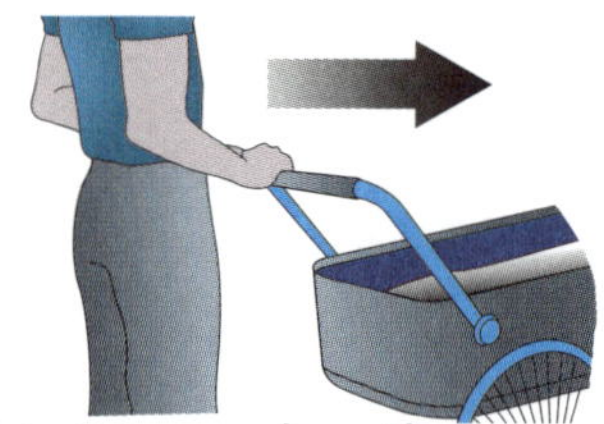
The man pushes the pram.

The Earth, like all other very massive objects, pulls everything else towards it.

- The force that pulls an object down towards the Earth is called its weight.
- Like all other forces, weight is measured in Newtons (N for short).

On the Earth the weight of each kilogram of material is about 10 N, so a 25 kg sack of potatoes is pulled towards the Earth with a force of 250 N.

Exercise 1

1 Write down four things that forces can do.

2 The force that pulls a child down is the child's weight.

Write a description of this force in the form *object A pulls or pushes object B.*

3 How much does a 60 kg woman weigh in Newtons?

4 Write a description of the force shown by the arrow on the diagram.

5 a When a crane lifts a heavy load, does it use a pulling or a pushing force?

b What other force acts on the heavy load?

Tactics

Always describe forces using a phrase such as object A pulls or pushes object B.

RED ALERT When an object floats on water, the upward push of the water is equal in size to the downward pull of the Earth.

Staying still

You are surrounded by things that are not moving, even though there are forces acting on all the objects that you can see.

Everything on this planet has at least one force acting on it – the Earth's pull.

If something is not moving there must also be another force pushing or pulling it so that the forces are balanced.

When you sit on a chair it changes shape; the springs and cushion get squashed so that they push up on you. You now have two equal-sized forces acting on you in opposite directions – the pull of the Earth and the push of the chair; the forces on you are balanced.

The diagram shows another example of balanced forces.

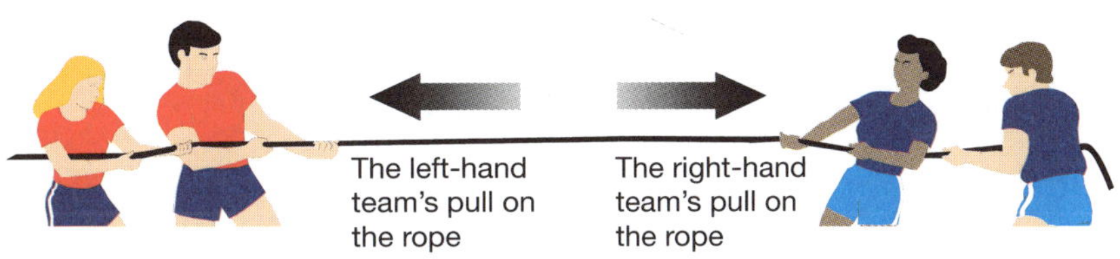

Floating and sinking

- If you push a plastic ball into a bucket of water you can feel the water pushing it back up – the more you push it in, the bigger the upward push of the water becomes.
- When a ball floats the forces on it are balanced; the upward push of the water is equal in size to the downward pull of the Earth.
- An object sinks if its weight is greater than the upward push of the water.

Exercise 2

1 Describe the force that acts on every object on the planet.

2 If an object is not moving, are the forces on it balanced or unbalanced?

3 When two balanced forces act on an object, how do they compare in:

  a size?

  b direction?

4 A plastic football floats on water.

  a Describe the forces acting on the football.

  b The football is pushed down and then released. Explain why it rises to the surface.

Tactics

Remember that when an object is not moving the forces acting on it are balanced; they are equal in size and opposite in direction.

Getting moving

To start or stop movement, to speed up or slow down, there needs to be an unbalanced force.

A train, a car, a bus, a bike and a person walking all need a force to make them move.

Two forces are shown on the diagrams of the cyclist:

- the force on the left diagram is the driving force that pushes the cycle along
- the force on the right diagram is the air resistance that acts against the cyclist's motion.

Anyone who has ever ridden a bicycle has felt the effect of air resistance; the faster you go, the bigger this resistive force gets.

When you are riding a bicycle there are always resistive forces.

- Most of the resistance to motion comes from the air.
- There are also resistive forces in places such as the wheel bearings that oppose a cyclist's motion.

Exercise 1

1 When a cyclist starts to move, are the forces on the cycle balanced or unbalanced?

2 As a cyclist speeds up, what happens to the size of the resistive force?

3 Which force pushes a cyclist along?

4 Which force opposes a cyclist's motion?

5 State two resistive forces that act on a moving cyclist.

Tactics

Most moving objects have both driving and resistive forces acting on them. The exceptions are objects that move through a vacuum; in this case there is no resistive force.

RED ALERT Air resistance acts against all objects moving through the air. There is no air resistance on objects that move in a vacuum.

Riding a bike

Driving and resistive forces are both at work on a moving cyclist.

- For the cyclist to speed up, the driving force needs to be bigger than the resistive force.
- If the resistive force is bigger than the driving force, the cyclist slows down.
- The only forces acting when the cyclist brakes are resistive forces.

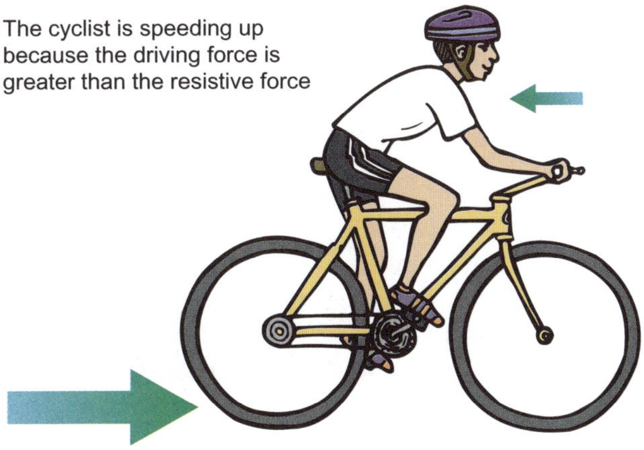

When you get on a bicycle and start to pedal:

- the resistive force is small at first so you speed up quite rapidly
- as your speed increases so does the resistive force
- eventually you get to a speed where the resistive force is equal in size to the driving force
- when this happens you stop speeding up and travel at a constant speed.

The forces acting on an object moving in a straight line at a constant speed are balanced. They are the same size but act in opposite directions so that their combined effect is just as if there were no force acting at all.

Exercise 2

1. When a cyclist is speeding up, which force is bigger, the driving force or the resistive force?
2. Describe what happens to the size of the resistive force acting on a cyclist as her speed increases.
3. Explain why there is no driving force acting when a cyclist brakes.
4. The forces acting on a moving cyclist are balanced. Describe the motion of the cyclist.
5. A car is travelling at a constant speed in a straight line along a level road. The driving force is 1200 N in the forwards direction. State the size and direction of the resistive force.

Tactics

The forces on an object are balanced when it is not moving or not changing its speed or direction.

Resistive forces

When you swim you have to work to push against the water; when you run you have to work to push against the air. You can probably run faster than you can swim because the resistive force from the air is less than that from the water.

The main resistive force on a moving car is air resistance.

There are other resistive forces that act on moving objects. Sometimes their effect is to slow down or stop the motion but they also make motion possible. Without resistive forces we cannot walk, and bikes, cars, buses and trains cannot move.

Friction is a resistive force that acts against sliding or slipping.

- If you push a book across a desk, friction is the force that slows it down and stops it.
- Friction always acts in the opposite direction to any sliding motion.
- Rough surfaces cause bigger friction forces than smooth ones, so if you want something to slide you should keep the surface smooth and polished or lubricated.

Ice is a good surface to slide on but a very poor surface to walk or ride a bike on.

Exercise 1

1 What do you push against when you:

a run?

b swim?

2 What force opposes slipping and sliding?

3 Explain why a resistive force cannot make an object move.

4 Explain why it is easier to slide on a polished floor than on an unpolished floor.

5 Why is it difficult to walk on ice?

Tactics

The forwards push of friction stops the wheels from slipping when you ride a bike.

RED ALERT

Friction and air resistance are different types of force. Friction opposes slipping and sliding. Air resistance opposes motion through the air.

How do resistive forces affect movement?

When we walk we rely on friction to stop our feet from slipping.

- To walk forwards our feet push backwards on the ground.
- The friction force stops them from moving backwards and pushes us forward.
- Without friction, our feet would just slip and we would not get anywhere!

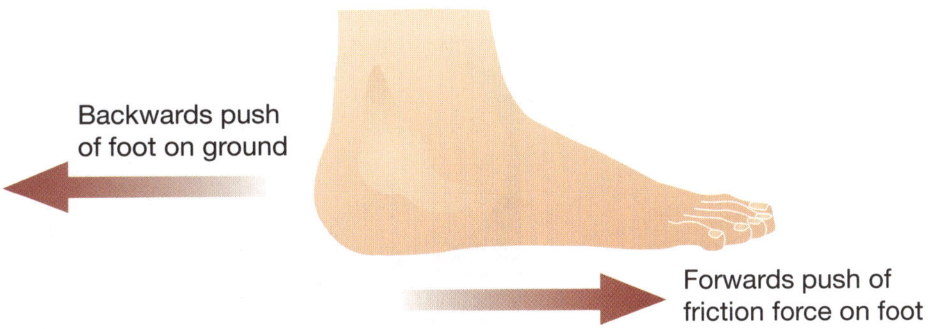

Trains also need friction between the wheels and the rails. When wet leaves get on the track the friction force is reduced and the train wheels slip.

Parachutists depend on resistive forces to slow them down. A sky-diver who jumps from an aircraft speeds up to a speed of about 60 metres per second. At this speed the air resistance balances the Earth's pull on the sky-diver. Opening the parachute causes the air resistance to get bigger, so the forces acting on the sky-diver are no longer balanced. The sky-diver now slows down.

Eventually the sky-diver falls at a much lower steady speed with the Earth's pull and the air resistance once again in balance.

Exercise 2

1 When we walk forwards, in which direction do our feet push on the ground?

2 Explain why trains cannot move if there are wet leaves on the track.

3 The diagram shows the forces acting on a sky-diver.

   a Write descriptions of the upward and downward forces that act on the sky-diver.

   b How can you tell that the forces on the sky-diver are balanced?

   c Explain why the resistive force on the sky-diver increases when the parachute is opened.

   d Describe and explain how the sky-diver's speed changes when the parachute is opened.

Tactics

A common error in Key Stage 3 tests is to state that a skydiver starts to move upwards when the parachute is opened.

The Solar System

If you could look at the Solar System from far off, at its centre you would see the Sun, shining with a brilliant white light. The Sun is the Solar System's star, the source of its light.

You would only be able to see half of each planet, because planets are only visible by the sunlight that they reflect and only the half of each planet facing the Sun would be lit up.

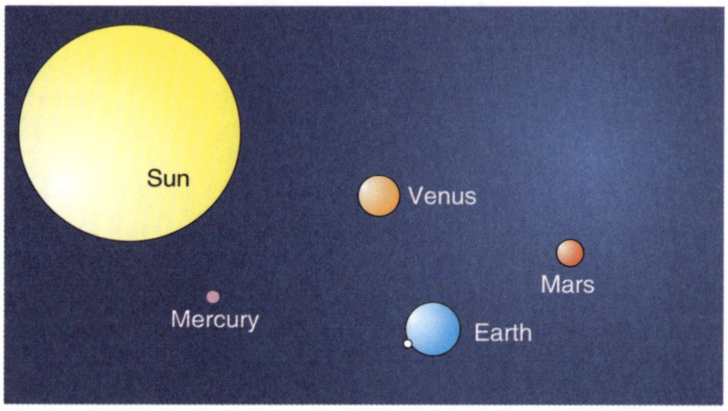

The inner planets

You would notice four planets close to the Sun:

- nearest to the Sun is the tiny planet Mercury
- next comes orange Venus
- the third planet is the blue planet Earth
- the fourth planet out from the Sun is Mars.

You would notice that the Earth has a satellite of its own, a moon. The Earth's moon takes about twenty eight days to complete an orbit of the Earth. It takes the same time to spin once on its axis, so the same side of the Moon always faces towards the Earth.

The Moon is kept in orbit around the Earth by the Earth's gravitational pull. Remember, the Moon also pulls the Earth with an equal-sized force that acts in the opposite direction. So, the Earth pulls the Moon and the Moon pulls the Earth.

Exercise 1

1 Which object is at the centre of the Solar System?

2 Explain how planets can be seen.

3 Suggest why Venus appears brighter than Mars when viewed from the Earth.

4 What objects are orbited by moons?

5 Explain why the view of the Moon seen from the Earth is always the same.

Tactics

Make up a phrase that helps you to remember the order of the planets.

RED ALERT The closer a planet is to the Sun, the shorter the time it takes to complete one orbit.

Beyond the inner planets

Moving your eyes further out, you would notice a lot of rocky fragments orbiting the Sun between Mars and the first of the outer planets, Jupiter. These fragments of rock, up to 100 km in diameter, form the asteroid belt.

The outer planets, in order from the Sun, are:

- Jupiter, the largest planet in the Solar System. It has a swirling atmosphere and sixteen moons.
- Saturn, the sixth planet, is a very bright yellow object in the sky. It has many rings around it.
- Uranus has rings and a total of fifteen satellites, five of which are large moons.
- Neptune, the eighth planet, is very similar in size and composition to Uranus.
- Pluto, the outermost known planet, has one known moon.

Planetary motion

Looking at the planets, you would see that:

- they all go round the Sun in the same direction
- the speed of a planet depends on its distance from the Sun
- Mercury moves fastest of all and it also has the shortest distance to travel to complete an orbit.

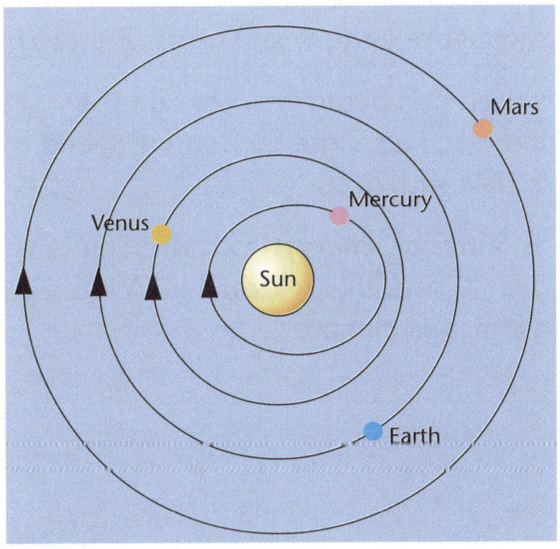

Pluto, the most distance planet, has the slowest orbital speed and greatest orbital distance. Of all the known planets, it takes the longest time to complete one orbit.

Exercise 2

1 Which planet's orbit is between that of Saturn and Neptune?

2 Which objects orbit the Sun between the inner planets and the outer planets?

3 Which two planets have rings?

4 Pluto is the only planet that has not been photographed close-up. Suggest why.

5 Give two reasons why it takes Pluto the longest time to orbit the Sun.

Tactics

You do not need to remember any details about individual planets, but you do need to know their relative positions.

The moving Earth

The Sun appears to move across the sky – rising in the East and setting in the West. This 'movement' of the Sun is actually due to the Earth turning round once each day. The Earth spins on its axis, an imaginary line going through the centre of the Earth from pole to pole.

The Earth makes one complete rotation on its axis in one day.

This daily rotation of the Earth causes day and night. The diagrams show Britain at sunrise, noon and sunset. This is the view you would have if you were looking down at the North pole. The outer circle of the Earth is the equator.

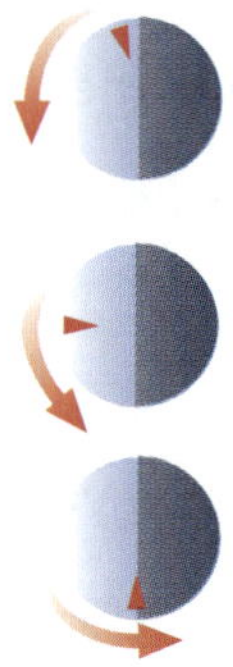

The number of hours of daylight and darkness varies throughout the year. This is due to the Earth being tilted.

When it is Summer in Britain the northern hemisphere is tilted towards the Sun, so we spend more than twelve hours in daylight.

In Summer, energy from the Sun is spread over a smaller area than in Winter, giving us a warmer climate.

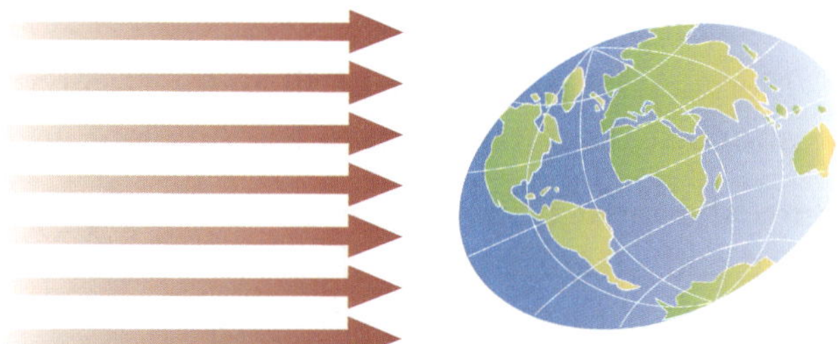

Exercise 1

1 What is the cause of the apparent movement of the Sun across the sky?

2 Draw a diagram that shows the position of Britain relative to the Sun at sunset.

3 What causes the number of hours of daylight to vary during the different seasons?

4 When it is Summer in the northern hemisphere, it is Winter in the southern hemisphere. Explain why.

5 Why is it warmer in Summer than in Winter?

Tactics

Remember that the Sun appears to be lower in the sky in winter than in summer.

RED ALERT The apparent movement of the stars is caused by the Earth spinning on its axis and rotating around the Sun.

Moving stars

The Earth's spin on its axis makes the stars in the northern sky appear to revolve anticlockwise around the Pole Star, making one complete revolution each twenty four hours. Stars in the southern sky appear to move round clockwise.

If the Earth's only movement was spinning on its axis, we would see the stars in the same place at the same time each night. But we have to take into account the movement around the Sun:

- as we revolve once around the Sun it looks as if the stars are turning once around the Pole Star
- since there are 365 days in a year and 360° in a circle, the pattern of the stars seems to move by about 1° each day
- if you look at the stars at the same time of night, in one month they should have moved round in the sky by about 30°.

Orion at 9 pm

Orion at 9 pm one month later

Star collections

A cluster of stars that make a pattern is called a constellation. In winter the constellation Orion can be seen in the southern sky. It appears to revolve around the Pole Star:

- by 360° each day because of the Earth's spin
- by 1° each day because of the Earth's movement around the Sun.

Exercise 2

1 Which star is always in the same position in the sky?

2 State two causes of the apparent movement of the stars.

3 How many complete revolutions do the stars appear to make around the Pole Star in a non-leap year? Explain your answer.

4 What is the shortest time that it takes for the stars in the group called the Plough to appear to rotate around the Pole Star by 180°? Explain why this could only be observed in winter.

Tactics

The Pole Star does not appear to move like the other stars. This is because the Earth's axis is pointing towards it.

1 The diagram shows a plant cell.

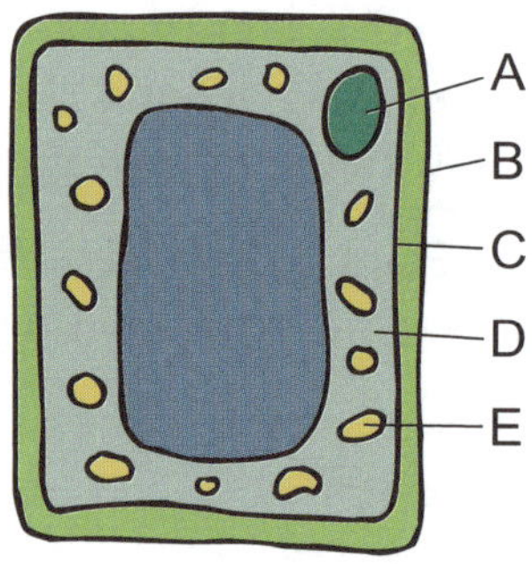

a Which TWO parts of the cell are not found in animal cells? [2]

____

b What is the name and job of part E? [2]

____

c In which part of the cell are the genes? [1]

____

2 The diagram shows a peppered moth.

Most peppered moths are grey. During the day they rest on tree trunks.

Explain how the peppered moth is adapted to survive in its environment. [2]

____

____

3 Choose words from the list to complete the sentences about the menstrual cycle.

an aviary an ovary cervix day fallopian month uterus vagina year

The menstrual cycle lasts approximately one ______________ .

After the lining of the uterus falls away and passes out through the ______________ , an egg ripens in ______________ .

This is released half way through the cycle and as it travels along the ______________ tube a new thick lining is forming in the ______________ . [5]

4 Sue finds some spilt liquid on the floor of the laboratory. She takes a sample of the liquid and tests it to find its pH value.

a What should she use to find the pH value of the liquid? [1]

____

The pH value of the liquid is 2.

b What does this tell her about the liquid? Put a ring around the best answer.

The liquid is:

strong acid **weak acid** **exactly neutral** **weak alkali** **strong alkali** [1]

c Suggest how she should neutralise and clean up this liquid. [2]

____

____

5 Kim heats a beaker containing ice cubes.

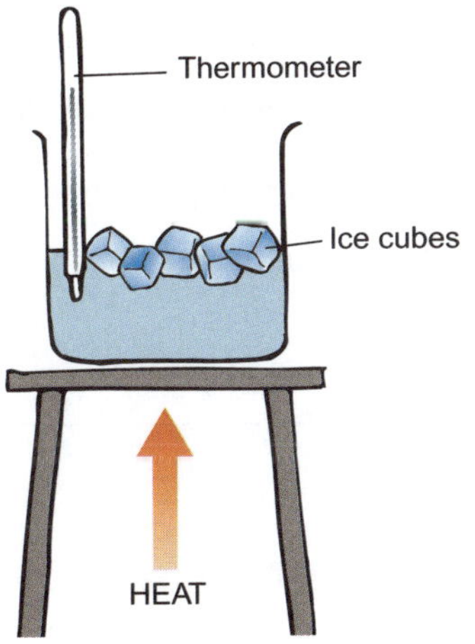

a i What happens to the ice cubes? [1]

____

ii Why is this a physical change? [1]

____

The outside of the beaker goes misty as small droplets of water are formed.

b Explain how this water is formed. [2]

____

____

6 The table gives the solubility of sugar at different temperatures.

Temperature (°C)	10	30	40	50	60
Solubility (g/100 g of water)	191	220	240	260	290

a What pattern is there in the solubility of sugar in water as temperature increases? [1]

____

b Predict the solubility of sugar at 20°C [1]

______________________________ g/100 g water

c Calculate the mass of sugar that would dissolve in 250 g of water at 40°C to make a saturated solution. Show your working out. [2]

_______________________________________ g

7 Most of the electricity in this country is generated by burning coal. Some modern power stations use biomass in the form of fast-growing trees.

a Explain which of these fuels is renewable. [1]

____

b What is the energy source for both fuels? [1]

____

c Coal is a fossil fuel. Name **two** other fossil fuels that can be burned to generate electricity. [1]

____

8 The diagram shows a circuit that consists of a battery and two lamps. Both lamps light, but lamp B is brighter than lamp A.

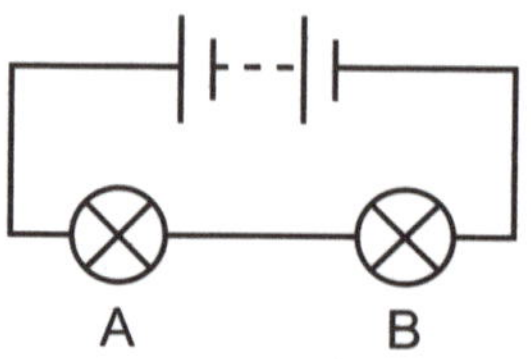

Sonja wants to measure the current in lamp A.

a What instrument should she use? [1]

____

b Draw the correct symbol for the instrument in the correct position on the circuit. [2]

c What is the job of the current in the circuit? [1]

____

9 The diagram shows the two horizontal forces acting on a car that is moving forwards.

a The table gives some values of these forces. Complete the table [2]

	Value of driving force in N	**Value of resistive force in N**	**Effect on speed of car**
i	750	250	
ii		600	None
iii	200	500	

b Which of the forces shown in the diagram:

i stops the wheels from spinning round?

____

ii is due to friction?

____

iii is mainly due to air resistance? [1]

____

c Explain why the driving force does not propel the car forwards when it travels over a patch of oil on the road. [2]

____

____

Answers to exercises

Unit 1 What are cells? (page 6)

Exercise 1

1 Chloroplasts and a cell wall.
2 The cell wall is tough.
3 Cellulose
4 **A** Cytoplasm **B** Nucleus **C** Cell membrane.

Exercise 2

1 The nucleus.
2 The cell needs to take in nutrients and get rid of waste.
3 Chlorophyll
4 Leaves contain chlorophyll to absorb energy from the Sun. Roots are not exposed to the Sun, so they have no use for chlorophyll.
5 Nutrients and waste products.

Unit 2 Building with cells (page 8)

Exercise 1

1 Cells 2 Tissue
3 **a** The heart. **b** The lungs.
c The brain. **d** The testes.

Exercise 2

1 To send information to and from the brain.
2 To move the eyeball.
3 Different parts of the eye do different jobs, each of which needs a different type of tissue.
4 Muscle tissue is needed to cause movement.

Unit 3 Specialised cells (page 10)

Exercise 1

1 The upper part of a leaf is exposed to direct sunlight; it needs chloroplasts to absorb energy from the Sun.
2 To take in water and minerals from the soil.
3 It has a large surface area.
4 A root hair cell is not exposed to light.

Exercise 2

1 The head.
2 To propel it.
3 They do not have to propel themselves.
4 Tiny hairs in the trachea.
5 To trap dust and bacteria.

Unit 4 Adolescence (page 12)

Exercise 1

1 Reproduction without sex involving one parent only.
2 A male sex cell and a female sex cell.
3 The child changes into an adult.
4 Hair grows around the penis and on the scrotum; the penis becomes larger.
5 Some plants can be grown from cuttings.

Exercise 2

1 To feed their young.
2 Once each month.
3 The hips broaden; breasts grow,
hair grows around the vulva.
4 The ovaries.
5 They want to appear attractive to other teenagers.

Unit 5 Menstruation (page 14)

Exercise 1

1 **a** The cervix. **b** The ovary. **c** The uterus.
2 The thickened lining falls away.
3 The womb.
4 It travels along the fallopian tube.

Exercise 2

1 28 days.
2 **a** The egg ripens. **b** In the ovary.
3 Between days 13 and 15.
4 The lining of the uterus is thickening.
5 **a** The lining of the uterus falls away.
b The egg has not been fertilised.

Unit 6 Fertilisation (page 16)

Exercise 1

1 The testes.
2 At the cervix.
3 To be at the correct angle to fit inside the vagina.
4 A male sex cell and a female sex cell fuse together.
5 One

Exercise 2

1 It travels along a fallopian tube.
2 An embryo is a ball of cells; a fetus has recognisable human features.
3 To keep it warm and protect it from shock.
4 Food, oxygen and waste materials.
5 To transfer materials between the blood of the mother and that of the fetus.

Unit 7 Habitats (page 18)

Exercise 1

1 The region where a plant or animal lives.
2 Food, shelter and a place to reproduce.
3 Dead leaves provide food.
The hedge shelters the ground from the weather.
The ground under the hedge provides a place to reproduce.
4 The woodland supports small animals for the fox to feed on.
5 Plants to provide food.

Exercise 2

1 It has fins to propel it through the water.
It has a tail to steer.
It has gills for gas exchange.
It has a streamlined shape.
2 It has strong hind legs so that it can run fast to catch its prey.
It has canine teeth for eating meat.
It has lungs for gas exchange.
3 There is more light on the woodland floor in spring, before the tree leaves are fully open.
4 Some can float on water others have long stems.

Unit 8 Feeding (page 20)

Exercise 1

1 Woodpecker
2 Plants make their own food, animals obtain their food from plants or other animals.
3 Water and carbon dioxide.
4 A herbivore only eats plants, a carnivore only eats other animals, an omnivore eats both.
5 The oak tree.

Exercise 2

1 They both increase in early summer and decrease during late summer.
2 The amount of rainfall and evaporation both vary.
3 To reduce the loss of heat and water.
4 By burrowing or as unhatched eggs.
5 There is more food available.

Unit 9 Different organisms (page 22)

Exercise 1

1 They reproduce sexually and breathe with their lungs.
2 Variation
3 Its parents.
4 All the nuclei are identical copies of the original cell that was formed at fertilisation.
5 No, since hair colour can be changed by dyeing it.

Exercise 2

1 Diet, exercise and physical activity.
2 a Both b Both c Genetic d Both
3 Both, since pigment is inherited but it is also affected by factors such as exposure to the Sun.

Unit 10 Classification (page 24)

Exercise 1

1 Plants 2 Protists
3 They are not made up of cells.
4 Asexually as there is only one parent.
5 So they can tell where each species fits into the pattern of life.

Exercise 2

1 Vertebrates have backbones, invertebrates do not.
2 Fish can only live in water, reptiles can live both on land and in water.
Fish have fins for movement, reptiles have legs.
Fish breathe using gills, reptiles use lungs.
3 Mollusca
4 Aves can fly, most Mammalia cannot.
5 Both are vertebrates.

Unit 11 What are acids and alkalis? (page 28)

Exercise 1

1 Sulphuric acid, nitric acid, hydrochloric acid, ethanoic acid, citric acid.
2 Sodium hydroxide, potassium hydroxide, calcium hydroxide, ammonia, bicarbonate of soda, washing powder, washing soda.
3 Alkali. Because it has hydroxide in the name.
4 Hydrogen

Exercise 2

1 Purple
2 **A** Acid **B** Alkali **C** Neutral
3 7 4 Orange 5 10

Unit 12 Neutralisation (page 30)

Exercise 1

1 To neutralise the acid.
2 pH increases slowly at first, then there is a rapid increase in pH. Finally the increase is slow again.
[Note: You are not describing the shape of the graph. It goes down slowly at first, then very quickly and finally slowly again.]
3 (a) C (b) A (c) D
4 Lemon juice.

Exercise 2

1 Wasp stings are alkaline and bee stings are acidic.
2 Nettle sting contains an acid and the alkali in dock leaves neutralises the acid.
3 An alkali such as lime.
4 There is the same amount of acid in each beaker. Fewer tablets will be needed for the brand containing more alkali.

Unit 13 Making new materials (page 32)

Exercise 1

1 a Chemical change. b Physical change.
c Chemical change. d Physical change.
e Physical change.
2 Manufactured: bricks, cement, glass, plastic, roofing tiles, steel; from the environment: stone blocks, wood.

Exercise 2

1 a Carbon dioxide. b Hydrogen
2 a Zinc b Sodium carbonate.
c Hydrogen d Carbon dioxide.
3 a Iron + **hydrochloric acid** → iron chloride + **hydrogen**.
b Sodium carbonate + hydrochloric acid → **sodium chloride** + **carbon dioxide** + **water**.

Unit 14 Burning (page 34)

Exercise 1

1 Oxygen
2 More air is trapped and so more oxygen.
3 Air
4 Dropping water removes heat. Cutting down trees removes fuel.

Exercise 2

1 Cardboard, newspaper, tree branches.
2 Petrol is flammable and a lit cigarette could ignite the petrol.
3 Zinc oxide.
4 To let air in for the magnesium to burn.

Unit 15 Solids, liquids and gases (page 36)

Exercise 1

1 0°C 2 100°C 3 Solid
4 Gas 5 Condensation

Exercise 2

1 Gas 2 Solid 3 Gas
4 If ice has its particles closely packed it should have a high density. Ice is an exception. It has a very open structure and is less dense than water. This is why it floats on water.

Unit 16 Solutions (page 38)

Exercise 1

1 72 g
2 a Copper sulphate solution.
b Blue
c Copper sulphate is the solute and water is the solvent.
3 Crushing the crystals into smaller pieces, heating the water and stirring. You could also use a larger volume of water.

Exercise 2

1 The other rocks do not dissolve in water, salt does.
2 Copper sulphate crystals.
3 Energy from the Sun.

Unit 17 Solubility (page 40)

Exercise 1

1 41 g 2 5.1 g 3 60°C 4 36 g
5 Crystals of potassium chloride.

Exercise 2

1 a 5.5 g b Sodium chloride.
c Alum d 68°C
2

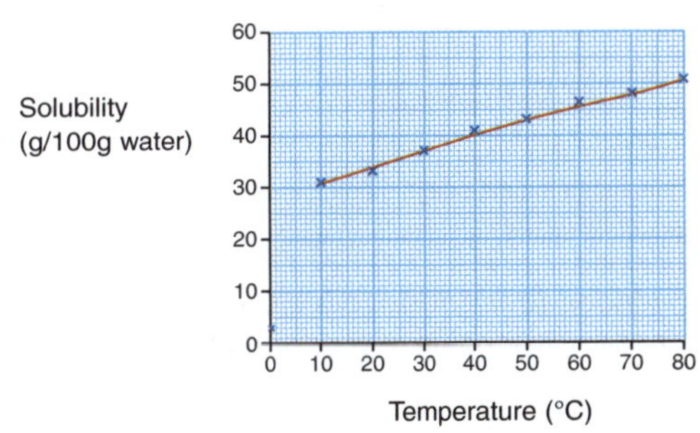

3 Since the solubility of sodium chloride is about the same at all temperatures, the cost of heating the water will not be recovered by more salt extracted.

Unit 18 Separating mixtures (page 42)

Exercise 1

1 Add the mixture of salt and sand to water. Stir. Salt dissolves and sand does not. Filter the mixture to remove the sand, which remains on the filter paper. Evaporate salt solution until salt remains.
2 100°C

3 To condense the steam.
4 So condensed water runs down into the flask.

Exercise 2
1 Three spots on the chromatogram above orange juice spot.
2 3
3 B, C and D.
4 If ink is used instead of pencil, the ink will start to separate into the dyes that make it up.

Unit 19 Mixing liquids (page 44)

Exercise 1
1 a Three b A, C, B (In order of density).
2 B G C E F A D.

Exercise 2
1 The boiling points are very close together. It is difficult to get a good separation.
2 a Ethanol b Whisky

Unit 20 Explaining with particles (page 46)

Exercise 1
1 Particles will move faster and so there will be more collisions with the walls of the container. This means a higher pressure.
2 Again there will be more collisions with the walls of the container and so a higher pressure.
3 When a piece of metal is heated the particles vibrate more and take up more space. This extra space can only come about if the solid expands, because the particles are very close together.

Exercise 2
1 Diffusion
2 The particles in a gas are moving much faster than the particles in a solid or liquid.
3 The particles are moving very rapidly and they have a very tiny mass because even when a large number escape, the perfume and bottle weigh almost the same.

Fuels and energy (page 50)

Unit 21 Where does our energy come from?

Exercise 1
1 Movement, heating and lighting.
2 Coal, oil and natural gas.
3 Coal 4 Oil and natural gas. 5 Wood

Exercise 2
1 So that the fuels last as long as possible.
2 The energy transferred to a house.
3 Joule (J)
4 500 J

Unit 22 Renewable resources (page 52)

Exercise 1
1 An energy resource that will not run out during the Earth's lifetime.
2 The wind.
3 The Moon (the Sun also has a small effect).
4 Plants are renewable energy resources that provide food for animals.
5 Hydroelectricity

Exercise 2
1 The installation costs are high and there are not enough hours of sunshine to provide a reliable source of hot water.
2 They do not produce enough electricity when it is needed most, at night and in cold weather they are expensive to install.
3 In rechargeable batteries.
4 Geothermal
5 There is no need to replace batteries.

Unit 23 Current in circuits (page 54)

Exercise 1
1 A complete current path from one terminal of the battery or power supply to the other terminal.
2 One
3 Three
4 a 
b 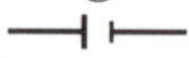
c 
5 Conductors: aluminium, brass, copper and steel.
Insulators: Perspex and polythene.

Exercise 2
1 Series 2 Parallel
3 a B
b Each lamp can be switched on and off without affecting the other one.

Unit 24 Electric current (page 56)

Exercise 1
1 The filament could be broken.
The current could be too small.
2 An ammeter.
3 Amp (A).
4 In series.
5 An analogue meter.

Exercise 2
1 a 2 A b None
2 To transfer energy from the power supply to the components.
3 Any two from: heat, infra-red radiation and light.
4 From the positive towards the negative terminal of the power supply.

Unit 25 Controlling the current (page 58)

Exercise 1
1 a It increases. b It decreases.
2 a Series b Change the speed of the motor.

Exercise 2
1 It decreases. 2 It increases.
3 A1 2.4 A A2 1.2 A A3 2.4 A

Unit 26 What do forces do? (page 60)

Exercise 1
1 Start things moving.
Stop things moving.
Change the direction or speed of a moving object.
Change the shape of an object.
2 The Earth pulls the child.
3 600 N
4 The girl pulls the door.
5 a A pulling force. b The Earth pulls the load.

Exercise 2
1 The Earth pulls each object downwards.
2 Balanced
3 a The sizes are equal.
b The directions are opposite.
4 a The Earth pulls the football down.
The water pushes the football up.
b The upward force from the water is greater than the downward force from the Earth.

Unit 27 Getting moving (page 62)

Exercise 1
1 Unbalanced
2 It increases.
3 The driving force (the push of the road on the tyres).
4 The resistive force.
5 Air resistance and resistance in the wheel bearings.

Exercise 2

1 The driving force.
2 The size of the resistive force increases with increasing speed of the cyclist.
3 The cyclist stops pedalling.
4 The cyclist moves at a constant speed in a straight line.
5 1200 N in the backwards direction.

Unit 28 Resistive forces (page 64)

Exercise 1

1 **a** The ground. **b** The water.
2 Friction
3 A resistive force can only oppose motion and acts in the opposite direction to any motion.
4 There is less friction on the polished floor as it is smoother.
5 There is not enough friction to stop the feet from slipping and sliding.

Exercise 2

1 Backwards
2 The wet leaves reduce the size of the friction force acting between the wheels and the track.
3 **a** The air pushes the skydiver upwards. The Earth pulls the skydiver downwards.
b The skydiver is moving at a constant speed.
c The air resistance increases due to the increased surface area.
d The speed decreases because the resistive force is greater than the Earth's pull.

Unit 29 The Solar System (page 66)

Exercise 1

1 The Sun.
2 They reflect light from the Sun and other stars.
3 Venus is closer to the Earth than Mars is, it is also closer to the Sun so is lit up more brightly.
4 Planets
5 The Moon spins on its axis once for each revolution of the Earth.

Exercise 2

1 Uranus
2 Asteroids
3 Saturn and Uranus.
4 It is the furthest planet away from the Earth. No space probes have yet been sent to it.
5 Pluto has the longest orbital distance and the slowest orbital speed.

Unit 30 The moving Earth (page 68)

Exercise 1

1 The Earth's rotation on its axis.
2

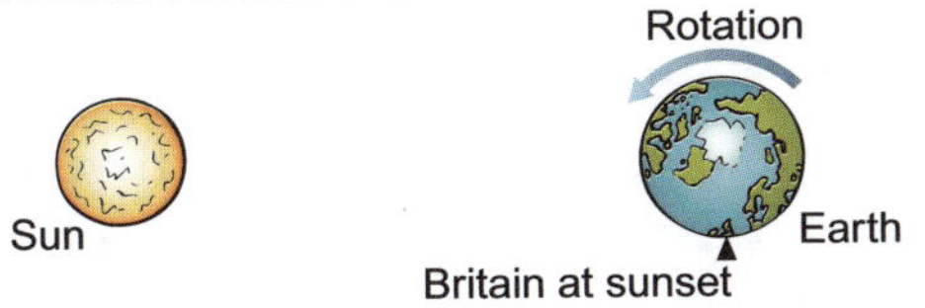

3 The Earth's tilt on its axis.
4 When the northern hemisphere is tilted towards the Sun, the southern hemisphere is tilted away from it.
5 Energy from the Sun is spread over a smaller area of the Earth.

Exercise 2

1 The Pole star.
2 The Earth's movement around the Sun and the Earth's rotation on its axis.
3 366, one for each day and one for one revolution around the Sun.
4 12 hours; nights at least this length are needed to be able to see it.

Answers to Year 7 Test Paper

1 **a** B and E (1 mark each). 2
b Chloroplast (1), to make food (1). 2
c A 1
2 It is a similar colour to the tree trunk(1), so not easily seen by birds who would eat it (1). 2
3 Month (1) vagina (1) an ovary (1) fallopian (1) uterus (1) 5
4 **a** Universal Indicator or pH meter. 1
b Strong acid. 1
c Add a weak alkali (such as bicarbonate of soda); wash away with plenty of water. 2
5 **a** **i** They melt. 1
ii The change can be reversed, ie water freezes to form ice 1
b Water is formed when gas burns. 1
Water condenses on the cold surface. 1
6 **a** As temperature rises solubility of sugar in water rises. 1
b Between 200 g and 210 g/100 g water. 1
c 2.5 x 240 1
600 g 1
7 **a** Wood, as more wood can be grown during the Earth's lifetime. 1
b The Sun. 1
c Oil and natural gas. 1
8 **a** An ammeter. 1
b Symbol, A in a circle (1).
Placed anywhere in series in the circuit (1). 2
c To transfer energy from the battery to the lamps. 1
9 **a** **i** Increases
ii 600
iii Decreases
All three correct
(1 mark for two correct). 2
b **i** Driving force.
ii Driving force.
iii Resistive force.
All three correct. 1
c There is less friction (1), so the driving force spins the wheels instead of moving thecar forwards (1). 2

Total marks: 36

Adolescence	the process of children growing into adults, which takes place in the early teenage years
Asexual reproduction	reproduction without sex
Boiling point	the temperature at which a liquid turns to a gas
Cells	the building blocks of all living things
Cellulose	the chemical which makes up the cell wall of a plant
Cell membrane	this holds the cell together and allows nutrients to pass in and waste products to pass out
Cell wall	a tough wall around a plant cell which keeps the cell in shape
Chemical change	produces a new material and it is impossible to turn the substance back to its original form. This is sometimes called permanent change.
Chlorophyll	a green chemical in chloroplasts found in plant cells. It absorbs energy from the Sun. This energy is needed for the plant to make food.
Chloroplasts	found in plant cells. Contain a green chemical called chlorophyll
Cilia	tiny hairs in the trachea (windpipe). The job of these hairs is to trap bacteria and dust so they do not enter the lungs.
Combustible	a substance that burns, e.g. wood, is said to be combustible
Combustion	burning, which is a chemical reaction that releases energy
Connective tissue	connects other types of tissue to form an organ
Cytoplasm	a mixture of chemicals in a cell including nutrition that has passed into the cell and waste products on their way out of the cell
Embryo	the first stage of development after an egg is fertilised
Fertilisation	the joining together of a male sex cell and a female sex cell
Fetus	an embryo that has developed to a point where it has recognisable human features
Flammable	a substance that catches alight easily is said to be flammable
Food chain	the feeding relationship in a habitat, where one type of creature feeds off another type, which in turn feeds off another, and so on, including some that feed off plants. Plants are always at the end of a food chain.
Freezing point	the temperature at which a liquid turns solid
Genetics	genetic information is contained in the male and female cells that join at fertilisation and determines the inherited characteristics of each living creature
Glucose	a simple sugar
Habitat	a community of plants and animals that depend on each other
Indicators	coloured solutions that can detect whether a substance is acid or alkali
Insoluble	a substance that does not dissolve is said to be insoluble
Invertebrates	animals without backbones
Litmus	an indicator which turns red if it is added to an acid, and blue if it is added to an alkali

JARGON BUSTER

Melting point	the temperature at which a solid turns to a liquid
Menstrual cycle	the process, each month, of an egg being released from an ovary and the womb lining thickening as it prepares itself to receive a fertilised egg
Muscle tissue	enables movement, for example, it moves the eyeball
Nerve tissue	sends information to the brain
Neutral solution	a solution which is neither acid nor alkali.
Nucleus	part of a cell that controls the actions of the cell
Organ	a part of the body, such as the heart or lung, which has a certain job to do
Organ system	a group of organs that work together to carry out a task
Ovaries	the organs from which female sex cells (ova) are released
Ovum	a female sex cell (an egg cell)
Oxides	substances formed when a material burns and uses up oxygen
Physical change	a change that can be reversed. This is sometimes called temporary change.
Placenta	an organ which grows within the uterus during pregnancy and enables food, oxygen and waste materials to be exchanged between the mother's blood and that of the fetus.
Property	a property of a material is a characteristic that the material has e.g. colour, density, conducts electricity
Sexual reproduction	a male sex cell joins with a female sex cell to create a new living thing
Soluble	a substance that dissolves is said to be soluble
Solute	the substance that dissolves in a liquid to form a solution
Solution	a new liquid formed when a substance dissolves in another liquid
Solvent	the liquid in which a substance dissolves is called the solvent
Species	a type of organism
Sperm	a male sex cell
Tissue	groups of cells that carry out a similar task. Each organ is made up of one or more different types of tissue.
Trachea	the windpipe, which is the tube through which we breathe, connecting the lungs to the nose and throat
Umbilical cord	joins the fetus to the placenta; food, oxygen and waste materials pass along the cord
Universal Indicator	a mixture of simple indicators that changes through a series of different colours to show the strength of an acid or alkali
Uterus	the organ of the female reproductive system in which the embryo and fetus develop. It is also known as the womb.
Vertebrates	animals with backbones

INDEX